ORGANIC FOOD GARDENING BEGINNER'S MANUAL

A complete guide to starting your own Organic Vegetable Garden

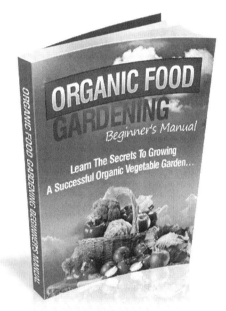

by Julie Turner

Join my **free** Go Organic Club and get weekly organic gardening articles, gifts, bonuses, reviews, and more at:

www.1stoporganicgardening.com/join.htm

Organic Food Gardening Beginner's Manual
Copyright © 2013 by Julie Turner.

This book is dedicated to all the ancestral lovers of gardening who
have contributed to the collective knowledge that is
Organic Gardening

ALL RIGHTS RESERVED.

ISBN: 978-1-4802-9220-8

Contents

Introduction

*T*hriving and productive organic vegetable gardens don't just happen. They are the result of planning, preparation and persistence.

Your organic garden will produce higher yields and more amazing results year after year, providing you pay attention to what works well in your garden and what doesn't. Like our gardens, our knowledge of gardening is a process undergoing constant change. That's one of the great things about organic gardening – you just keep learning.

But first off, let me congratulate you on deciding to go organic! By committing the time and effort required, you will find the rewards to be well worth it.

The benefits of eating fresh, chemical free, live foods, rich in vitamins and minerals are obvious.

Some other benefits you may not have considered are the health benefits of exercising, being in the sun (vitamin D) and fresh air, being able to go outside and pick what you want for your meal, interacting with other family members in the garden, stress/anxiety release, recycling of organic materials, leaving a smaller footprint on the environment... you get the idea!

So what is the difference between **ordinary** gardening and **organic** gardening? Basically organic gardeners choose to garden in harmony with nature, by using natural and organic materials and practices. We avoid using synthetic chemicals and fertilizers at all costs.

This way we are as kind to our health and the environment as possible. It is a holistic approach to gardening, where all elements and their interaction with other elements are observed and taken into consideration.

We use simple systems and techniques in our gardens that have nature helping us – such as:-

- No-Dig plots (encourages earthworms and micro-flora)
- Raised beds (to improve drainage and soil conditions)
- Companion planting (encouraging beneficial insects and vigorous growth)
- Composting (providing nutrient-rich humus)
- Liquid fertilizers (feeding our plants)
- Organic sprays (protecting plants without chemicals)
- Choosing the right location

The information found throughout these pages will be useful for all gardeners, but is written with beginners to organic practices and methods in mind.

Please don't feel intimidated by the list above. There is nothing difficult about any of these methods. They are all quite simple. It's really just a matter of having a go and practice.

A lot of organic gardening is about trying something, seeing how it goes, making a record of it in your journal and then modifying it if it didn't quite do what you wanted or expected it to.

First Things First – Planning

*P*lanning is the best way to achieve the results you want from your organic garden. The first thing you need to do is ask yourself a few questions to work out the needs of your family.

You can start by thinking about the size of your family and the amount of produce you are able to freeze, can, preserve, pickle, turn into jams, jellies, soups, sauces, chutneys etc. and store – as well as how much fresh produce you will need.

What vegetables, fruits, herbs and nuts does my family enjoy the most? There's no point growing cauliflower if no-one likes cauliflower! Make a list of what fruit and vegetables your family likes and uses most in the kitchen.

OK, now write it all down. Yes a list of all the things you'd like to grow for your family and roughly how much of each thing you would use per week.

You also have to decide what space you have available for your food plots. Obviously if you live in an apartment you will have more space limitations than someone living on acreage.

If you are limited for space, consider growing things that you use the most and things that are expensive to buy. More on limited space at page 77 in the chapter on Food Gardening In Small Spaces.

Choosing The Right Location

As with investing in real-estate, a highly productive vegetable garden relies on location, location, location. It is **the most important thing** to consider. You need to give quite a lot of consideration to the location of your main vegetable plots.

Many poor soil conditions can be corrected over time, but your number one priority should be **how much sun** the area receives – especially if you are lucky enough to be able to grow winter veggies. Having said that, make sure you read the next chapter on How To Create Healthy, Fertile Soil as this is an extremely important step if you want good yields and healthy plants.

You want to aim for an area that gets **at least six hours sunlight** each day. If you live in a temperate zone like I do, then I prefer to position the garden so that the maximum sunlight is from the morning. I don't mind too much if there's some afternoon shade through summer as our summers are very hot (35°C - 45°C, that's 95°F - 114°F) and dry.

You don't want to have large trees too close. They will create too much shade and compete with your vegetables for available nutrients and water.

The second most important issue is **water**. Your veggie garden must have access to a reliable water supply. Most of us have mains water available straight from the tap. This is really important as it can get really tiresome carting bucket load after bucket load to keep your garden alive. Besides, you don't want to just keep it alive – you want it to thrive.

If you have some kind of rainwater collection, that's even better. You may need to install a pump though, rather than rely on gravity fed if you are using an irrigation system. Gravity may work, so you will need to test this as it will be different for every garden, depending on how you plan to

4

water.

Grey water (or recycling household water) should be reserved for fruit and nut trees, lawn or ornamentals, unless your water goes through some sort of filtration system. Don't use it on your vegetables, herbs or soft fruits (fruits not grown on trees, such as berries, kiwi fruit, grapes etc.) unless you have had it tested for safety.

You also need to consider **how windy** your vegetable garden area may be. Some plants really dislike wind, so if you live in a windy area, are you able to erect a wind-break to reduce prevailing winds? I've had tomatoes grown in a wire cage topple over after reaching 2metres / 6feet. It's very disheartening.

Consider putting up something that reduces the wind, rather than totally blocking it. When you build a structure that blocks the wind, it creates a lot of turbulence that might have the opposite effect than what you're expecting and needing.

Instead you could use several layers of trees and shrubs. Or for something quicker, a sturdy trellis that could double as support for a food producing vine, such as kiwi fruit or passionfruit if they are suitable for your area.

These options reduce the amount of wind, without the turbulence.

The next thing to consider is **your soil**. Your soil needs to be (or become) a well-drained, loamy soil with a pH of about 6.5. Now if that means nothing to you, don't despair as we'll be talking a lot about simple ways to improve you soil and give your plants what they need in the next chapter.

Making soil amendments or improvements is an ongoing thing in an organic garden. Most of this is achieved with compost and the addition of organic matter. Don't worry, even the most difficult soils can be improved over time.

Finally, you might consider having your vegetable garden or main plot/s **close to your home** (especially the kitchen) – just for convenience. You don't want to have to run too far to grab the herbs to add to your dinner that's bubbling away on the stove.

I've moved house a few times, but I always seem to be lucky enough to have the right conditions for my veggie garden to be close enough to the house and right next to the chicken yard; just how I like it.

Your Garden Design

It really helps to draw your plans out on paper. You can include your house, shed/s, paths, driveways and any other structures, trees or shrubs. Think about any food plots that you'll want to grow perennials in.

Perennials are plants that grow for many years, not just one season. Such as rhubarb, asparagus, artichokes, grapes, perennial beans, many herbs and all of the fruit trees. Perennial plants are wonderful as they don't need much attention once they're established, but give you abundant food for many years.

Having your perennials in their own bed/s makes a lot of sense.

Then you can mark in where your seasonal vegetable plots can go – bearing in mind all the things you need to consider above.

Once you've decided on where things will go, it pays to stand and look at those areas at different times throughout the day (and year if you can wait that long) to make sure there is as much sunlight as you thought for that area.

Graph Your Garden Plot

Use the grid area below to graph out your garden for appropriate size and spacing. Use whatever scale is appropriate for your property ie. 1 square = 1 foot or 1 meter.

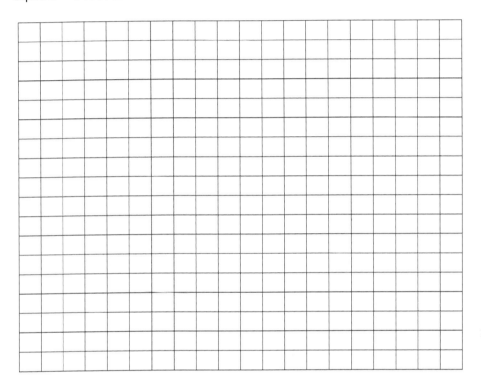

1. Print the graph out to work with, or draw up your own to the scale you need.

2. Draw the perimeter (border) of your property first. If you're not sure of the measurement, pace it out and count one pace as 1 metre or yard. It doesn't have to be exact, but close enough to give you a good estimation. Draw the northern border of your property at the top of your plan – so North is up.

3. Then draw on your house, driveway, paths, sheds and any other existing buildings or landscaping features. You can even include large trees, existing plant borders and lawn areas.

4. From your map so far you can now tell where areas of shade and sunlight are, plus you will be verifying this by physically standing in various parts of your yard at different times of the day.

5. Now you can draw in potential plots for your vegetables, herbs, perennials, fruit trees and soft fruits – you plan to grow. You can plan them to go over existing lawn if you want to reduce the amount of lawn you have (a good environmental choice). You can even build a raised bed over concrete if you're prepared to bring in soil.

Once you've decided on where your plots are going and what size they are, you need to print out another graph (or draw your own) to plan what plants you will put in and where.

You need to make the scale of this plan much smaller. Whereas your property plan might be 1cm square = 1metre or yard, your plot plans might be 10cm squares = 1 metre or yard. Otherwise everything will look so cramped that you won't even be able to read it properly.

This plan will depend on the time of year you are planning for. Most gardeners will spend the majority of their planning for the growing season. For most, this will be spring.

What tends to happen in my vegetable garden is that I start with a planting plan for mid spring (once the risk of frost has passed). Then as I complete harvesting for particular plants (for example corn) I pull out the spent plants, chop the stalks up and throw them on the compost heap, and fill the space with new plantings. This could be a second lot of lettuce, carrots and spring onions. Or it may be more beetroot, leeks and cucumber or zucchini.

Before I know it, it is late summer and I'm starting off seedlings of winter veggies, such as cauliflower, pak choy, more lettuce, broccoli, onions etc, ready to go into the space where tomatoes, capsicum, watermelon or whatever have finished.

Rotating your crops is also a good practice. Otherwise you will deplete the soil of particular nutrients / elements that the same crop planted continually in the same place uses. This also means that the crop will perform worse each year as the nutrients it needs decline and is more susceptible to disease.

You also need to know the right time of year to plant different families. For example: Cucurbits (cucumbers, squash, pumpkins, melons) need to grow in warm temperatures and need a long growing season to mature.

In winter (unless you can artificially provide the right conditions) a cucurbit crop would fail – so leave it till the ground has warmed, the days are lengthening and the risk of late frost has passed (mid spring in most areas).

I like to spend winter evenings **planning** what, where and how much I'm going to plant in my veggie garden next growing season.

Keeping a gardening journal comes in really handy when I'm planning. It reminds me what worked previously, what I'd like to do differently and whether or not I planted enough or too much of a particular plant to meet our family's needs.

So let's assume you're planning a spring vegetable plot. Easy to grow plants you might include when you're first starting out (if your family likes to eat them) are:

- Bush Beans
- Capsicum (peppers)
- Corn
- Lettuce (I mostly use the non-hearting varieties)
- Potatoes
- Pumpkin (try butternut or Japanese pumpkin from seeds)
- Radish
- Silverbeet
- Spring Onions
- Tomatoes - try growing a few basil plants close to your tomatoes
- Zucchini

This gives you plenty of variety to start out with. As you become more confident you will try more and more plants and different varieties.

For example, you have worked out that your entire family loves cucumbers. So you decide to plant several continental cucumbers, then say a few weeks later you plant apple cucumbers, then a few weeks after that you might put in some Lebanese cucumbers and perhaps grow an heirloom variety, just for curiosity. My personal favourite is an heirloom cucumber variety called "Armenian" – it's delicious and the cucumbers are really long and crunchy.

How To Create Healthy, Fertile Soil

Please don't skip over this section, because the health and vitality of your garden depends greatly on the soil it grows in.

*I*n your organic garden it is very important to have fertile soil to create the best possible growing conditions for healthy, tasty vegetables and great yields. Soil fertility is best when essential nutrients are available to your plants and when the humus levels are at 5% or more.

Humus is the stable decomposed remains of plant tissue. It is a product of composted vegetable matter, or if you like, your mature compost. The cellulose in humus acts like a sponge and holds moisture in the garden soil, making it available for growing plants, creating better drought tolerance. It has a water-holding capacity of up to five times its own weight.

It helps prevent water-soluble nutrients from being leached from the soil via watering or rainfall by binding itself to the nutrients, but at the same time making them available to plant roots.

It helps bring about a loose, crumbly structure in heavy clay soils, while allowing free drainage during excessive rain; and provides cohesion in sandy soils.

So you see that humus is really the best way to overcome whatever problems you may have with your soil. Humus is also necessary to maintain healthy levels of essential soil organisms, fungi, bacteria and earthworms.

Making your own compost is an integral part of organic gardening.

Sandy soils

Sandy soil has large, freely draining particles. Any nutrients present are quickly leached by watering and / or rainfall.

If you have sandy soil you will need to apply to the surface, or dig in, large amounts of humus to retain water and provide nutrients. All organic matter breaks down over time, so sandy soils will benefit from a large amount of compost, which will need replacing regularly.

Always mulch well to reduce evaporation. Did you know that a 20cm (4 inch) layer of mulch can reduce evaporation by up to 70%?

Sandy soils can become non-wetting soils, where any amount of irrigation will just run across the surface. If your soil is like this, you will need to add copious amounts of organic matter to correct this nasty problem.

Some organic soil wetting agents include vegetable soaps, plant and seaweed extracts and microbial wetting agents. When you're buying a wetting agent, just check to see if it's certified organic. Then you know that it's safe to use on your garden.

Clay soils

Clay soils are made up of tiny particles. It will hold water well, but the spaces between the soil particles are so small, there's little room for air, or space for water to escape. Clay soils tend to become boggy in wet weather, and dry out and crack in hot, dry weather. Clay soils often have high reserves of mineral elements, but roots are unable to mine them from the clay.

Gypsum is a well known clay breaker. Dig it into the soil for good effect. The clay will become friable and can then be made more workable by incorporating river sand and organic matter. You may want to construct raised beds to increase drainage.

Testing Your Soil

So what kind of soil do you have? Most soils are somewhere between the two extreme soil conditions above. A very simple, but effective way to test your soil is to use a glass jar. Add a handful of your soil, fill it with water and shake vigorously. Let it stand untouched for a few hours (or overnight) until all the suspended materials have settled. You will see quite distinct layers.

Course sand will be the lowest layer, then finer sands, silts, clays and lastly organic matter.

A good garden loam will have approximate equal proportions of clay, sands and silt, with a good percentage of humus or organic matter.

These jars are samples from my own yard. The sample on the left is from my vegetable plot, which has been built up with compost and organic matter. The layers are not so clear in the photo, but it is very good soil.

The sample on the right is the soil I started with here on this property – taken from an area where I haven't made any improvements. You can clearly see the bottom layer is very distinct and is mostly course sand, the rest being a small amount of clay and organic material. This is very difficult soil to work with as any watering just runs over the surface, without penetrating the soil.

If you have this type of soil I would recommend creating raised beds and bringing in loam with a generous top layer of compost. That way you'll have excellent drainage and fertile soil for your plants to thrive in.

Soil pH

The acidity or alkalinity of your soil is also an important consideration. The measuring of the acid / alkaline balance is called pH. The scale is from 1, being very acid, to 14, being very alkaline. 7 on the pH scale is considered neutral.

Most vegetables need a neutral to slightly acidic soil for optimum growth, with a pH of about 6.5. If your soil pH isn't right, then some nutrients will be unavailable to your plants. It really is a good idea to find out the pH of your soil so that you can correct it if necessary.

You can buy a pH testing kit at your local nursery or hardware store – they are cheap, very easy to use and can be used over and over. They come with full instructions. You will need to test your vegetable patch every year. Plus it will come in handy when you include other food plants with specific pH preferences.

If you discover that your soil is particularly acidic, say around pH5, you can add lime or dolomite (lime and magnesium) to bring up the pH. If your soil is too alkaline, around pH8 or higher, you will need to add iron sulphate or flowers of sulphur. You can also reduce alkalinity by adding leaf-mould, peatmoss or old pine needles.

If you're starting with bare soil just follow the instructions on the whatever product you are using. But if there are already plants growing where you need to amend your soil, you will need to do it in stages so that you don't shock the existing plants.

The really great news is that no matter what kind of soil you are starting with, the continued addition of humus and other organic materials will correct nearly ever problem kind of soil. Even your pH levels will balance out over time.

Preparing Your Soil Before Planting

Organic fertilizer and soil conditioning materials can take a while to be effective. To make sure they are doing the job you want them to, they should be mixed into the soil at least three weeks ahead of planting.

Another thing to be aware of, is that any organic materials that are not properly composted can actually absorb nutrients from the soil as they continue to break down, robbing your young seedlings of precious and essential nutrients. This can sometimes result in nutrient deficiency and possible soil-borne diseases problems such as "damping-off" of your young seedlings.

So make sure your compost is mature before adding it to your garden. You can do this by grabbing a handful (yes, it's wonderful).

If it feels quite hot in your closed hand it needs to be turned over and allowed a little longer to "cook". Mature compost won't be hot in your hand. It will smell sweet and earthy and have a fairly even texture.

Feeding Your Soil

*F*eeding your soil organic matter is one of the foundations of gardening the organic way. By adding organic nutrients to the soil we are emulating nature. The ways that we can provide nutrients organically to the soil include adding mature or well composted animal manures, green manure cover crops, mulch, compost, or mixed organic fertilizer.

It is a critical step to growing food organically to maintain a supply of nutrients ready for your plants to take up as they need them. This way your plants will grow vigorously, which helps prevent attacks of pests and disease. It also means that you will benefit from higher yields and quicker growing times.

Benefits Of Building Up Your Soil With Organic Matter

1. Improvement of the condition and structure of your soil;
2. Improves the ability of your soil to hold water;
3. Provides additional nutrients to the soil;
4. Allows nutrients to be released slowly;
5. Improve the soil's microbiological activity;
6. Releases insoluble natural additives such as ground rock into plant-usable forms;
7. Helps dispose of your organic waste materials.
8. Encourages earthworms and micro-organisms.

Make Your Own Compost

So Why Make Compost?

*T*here are so many benefits to creating your own compost that I think it's not only worth the effort, but an integral part of your organic gardening system.

1. Wherever you make your well made compost heap it will get so hot that the soil underneath it 'burns', along with any weeds – so it will even kill Couch or Kikuya grass. Native soil life can bury down under the hot surface area to survive. Enough nutrients leach down into the soil under the heap for them to feed on. This area under your compost pile becomes a very fertile, cleared planting bed – too good to waste by building the next compost pile in the same place. Consider building your next compost pile where you want your next planting area.

2. Compost gives an initial quick boost to the population of soil micro-organisms when you are first establishing an area. Using compost to plant out (at least for the first time) provides your garden beds with starter cultures of micro-organisms.

3. Use your compost to create your own seedling raising and potting mixes. Combined with worm castings and river sand, compost based seedling raising mix has the right texture, water retaining and draining qualities and is nutrient-rich enough to

give seedlings and cuttings a great start.

4. To provide additional nutrients in the garden when planting out heavy feeders following another heavy feeder.

5. To incorporate organic matter into the garden that isn't suitable for feeding to the chickens. So many household and garden materials can go into creating wonderful nourishment for your plants that would have to be otherwise disposed of. By turning it into compost instead, you are greatly reducing the burden on the environment while keeping yourself fit in the process.

6. Compost is often used as a nutritious layer of mulch, reducing evaporation and helping keep down the weeds.

The Simple Science of Making Compost

Compost is a living culture – a colony of micro-organisms that convert organic matter into humic acid, locking up nutrients in large molecules that are not readily water-soluble.

This means that they don't leach out of the soil like soluble fertilisers do, and that the nutrients are not 'force-fed' to your plants as they take in water. Plants can absorb and digest these nutrients with their feeder roots, taking just what they need for healthy growth.

Making compost is a process of cultivating micro-organisms. As with all living things, for them to do well they have specific needs which have to be met. Your compost heap will flourish if the micro-organisms are given enough water, air, carbon-rich food, not too much nitrogen-rich food, micro-nutrients, an acid environment and heat.

- Water comes from wetting down each layer of the pile

when making (and turning).

- Air comes from allowing holes in the pile, using some ingredients that are bulky (providing air pockets), not compressing the pile and turning it over etc.

- Carbon-rich food comes from dry-ish or woody plants like hay, straw or dried leaves, cardboard and paper.

- Nitrogen comes from green plant materials (such as lawn clippings, comfrey, azolla and legumes) animal manures and human urine. (Urine needs to be diluted and allowed to stand for 24 hours before use).

- Micro-nutrients come from mixing in as broad a variety of materials as possible, including herbs, weeds, seaweed and waterweeds.

- The acidic environment occurs on its own accord, providing you do not add lime, dolomite or wood ash to your pile.

- Heat is generated by the compost micro-organisms themselves. You need to help conserve it. You can do this by having the minimum surface area – the best shape that does this is a sphere, but a dome shape is close enough.

WHAT CAN I COMPOST?

If it can rot it will compost, but some items are best avoided. Some things, like grass clippings and soft young weeds, rot quickly. They work as 'activators' or 'hotter rotters', getting the composting process started, but on their own will decay to a smelly mess.

Older and tougher plant material is slower to rot but gives body to the finished compost - and usually makes up the bulk of a compost heap. Woody items decay very slowly; they are best chopped or shredded first – the smaller the ingredient, the quicker it will break down.

For best results, use a mixture of many types of ingredients. The right balance is something you will learn with experience.

Compost ingredients

Activators
- Comfrey leaves
- Yarrow
- Young weeds
- Grass cuttings
- Chicken manure
- Pigeon manure
- Human Urine

A balanced diet
- All biodegradable kitchen waste
- Tea bags
- Coffee grounds
- Old flowers
- Bedding plants
- Old straw & hay
- Vegetable plant remains
- Strawy manures
- Young hedge clippings
- Spent hops
- Feathers
- Seaweed (Kelp preferably – washed)
- All nut shells and husks
- Egg shells
- Prawn heads, crab & crayfish shells
- Vacuum cleaner dust
- Human & animal hair and nail clippings
- Soft prunings
- Perennial weeds

- Gerbil, hamster & rabbit bedding

Other compostable items
- Cotton rags (unprinted)
- Cheesecloth
- Cardboard (not waxy or printed)
- Jute bags, Hessian and Canvas
- Paper towels & bags
- Butchers' paper
- Cardboard tubes
- Egg cartons (not plastic or styrofoam)

Slow cookers - very slow to rot
- Autumn leaves
- Tough hedge clippings
- Woody prunings
- Sawdust
- Wood shavings
- Old under-felt (not chemically treated)

Do NOT compost
- Coal & coke ash
- Cat or Dog litter & feces
- Disposable diapers (nappies)
- Glossy paper or magazines

What type of heap to build?

You can make compost simply by adding compostable organic items to a compost heap when you feel like it. It will all rot eventually but it can take a long time, may not produce a very pleasant end product, and could smell.

With a little extra attention - taking the 'COOL HEAP' option outlined here - you could improve things dramatically.

If you want to produce more compost in a much quicker time, and are able to put a little more effort into it, follow the 'HOT HEAP' option.

The Cool Heap

1. Collect together a batch of compost materials. Try, if possible, to get enough to make a layer a minimum of 30cm / 12inches or more in the compost bin. Weed the garden, mow the lawn, empty the kitchen scrap bucket; whatever it takes!

   Aim for a mix of soft and tough items. It may help if you place a few woody plant stems or small twigs on the bottom first, especially if using a plastic bin, as this will improve the air circulation and drainage.

   Go to Step **2**, or jump to the 'HOT HEAP' Step **2** if you can make the time.

2. Start filling the bin. Spread the ingredients out to the edges. Alternate soft and tough items, or mix them together first. Unless items are already wet, water well every 30-60cm.

3. Continue to fill the container. Items can be added individually, but a bigger batch is preferable. If most of what you compost is kitchen waste, mix it with egg boxes, kitchen paper, loo roll middles and similar paper products to create a better balance.

   Go to Step **4**, or take a detour via the 'HOT HEAP' Step **4** on the way if you are energetic enough to turn it.

4. When the container is full - which it may never be as the contents will sink as it composts - or when you decide to, stop adding to it. Then either just leave it to finish composting or go to Step **5**.

5. Remove the container, or everything from the container. If the lower layers have composted, use this on the garden. Mix everything else together well; add water if it is dry, or add more dry material if it is soggy. Replace in the bin and leave to mature.

The Hot Heap

1. Gather enough material to fill your compost container or area in one session. Bring in manure, scraps from the market, neighbours' weeds and so on to make up the bulk. Make sure you have a mixture of soft and tough materials.

2. Chop up tough items using shears, a sharp spade (lay items out on soil or grass to avoid jarring) or a shredder / mulcher.

3. Mix ingredients together as much as possible before adding to

the container. In particular, mix items, such as grass clippings, that tend to settle and exclude air, with more open items that tend to dry out. Fill the container as above, watering as you go.

4. Give the heap a good mix.

5. Within a few days, the heap is likely to get quite hot to the touch. When it begins to cool down, or a week or two later, turn the heap. Remove everything from the container or lift the container off and mix it all up, trying to get the outside to the inside. Add water if it is dry, or dry material if it is soggy. Replace in the bin.

6. The heap may well heat up again with the new supply of air you have mixed in. This allows the fast-acting aerobic microbes, ie those that need oxygen, to continue with their work. Step **4** can be repeated several more times if you have the energy, but the heating will tend to be less and less.

When your compost no longer heats up again, leave it undisturbed to finish composting.

When is it ready?

Compost can be made in six to eight weeks depending on what time of year, or it can take a year or more. In general, the more effort you put in, the quicker you will get compost.

When the ingredients you have put in your composting container have turned into a dark brown, earthy smelling material, the composting process is complete.

It is then best left for a month or two to 'mature' before it is used. Don't worry if your compost is not fine and crumbly. Even if it is lumpy, sticky or stringy, with bits of twig and eggshell still obvious, it is quite usable.

Tips To Really Get Your Compost Heap Cooking

It seems that most organic gardeners love the idea of making their own compost, but some gardeners have trouble making it really happen. Don't give up! There are ways to give your compost heap a boost and get it heating up again – creating beautiful, nutritious humus for your veggie garden.

OK, so after six months your 'compost' has remained unchanged from it's original state? Remember there are certain conditions your heap needs to be able to actively turn it's ingredients into compost. They are air and moisture. Here are some things you can try.

1. Turn your heap over, exposing it to air, watering if dry.
2. If your heap dries out it will stop breaking down. Water the heap every few days in summer if conditions are hot and dry.
3. Add ingredients that are as small as possible. Use a shredder, mulcher or lawn mower to chop up larger ingredients such as prunings and larger leaves.
4. To speed up the composting process add lots of nitrogen-rich ingredients such as clover, manure laden straws, herbal activators (see below), washed sea-weed or fishmeal.

Herbs As Compost Activators – some herbs are well known as particularly impressive compost activators. Add them to your heap to speed up your results.

Comfrey *(Symphytum officinale)* is rich in calcium, nitrogen, phosphates and potassium. It has large hairy leaves that break down very quickly.

Dandelion *(Taraxacum sp)* also accelerates the breaking down of materials in the heap. It is rich in copper, potash and iron, all valuable goodies in your compost.

Valerian *(Valeriana officinalis)* has a reputation for attracting earthworms to the compost heap. Its leaves are also rich in minerals.

Yarrow *(Achillea sp)* can have the most dramatic effect in your heap, even in small amounts. It will enrich your compost with nitrates, potash, phosphates and copper, so is a very valuable addition.

Tansy *(Tanacetum vulgare)* has the ability to concentrate potassium from the soil where it grows. Adding Tansy to your compost means adding potassium.

If you have the room, it's best to have two or more compost piles on the go. One that you are preparing by gathering materials, one that is semi-matured and one that has already turned into that gorgeous, black, earthy plant tonic – ready to use.

One more tip is to make sure air can get to the middle of your heap, especially if you don't plan to turn it often. Place garden stakes or pvc pipes through the middle of your heap so that you can 'jiggle' them every few weeks allowing air to get to the centre of your heap.

Try some of these tips and I'm sure you will speed things up for your compost heap and you will be topdressing your veggies with your own compost in no time.

You don't need to race out and buy hundreds of dollars worth of brand new gardening tools to get started. But you will need the basics. If you've got a shed, then chances are you've already got some of the tools you will need to start your organic veggie garden.

Firstly, there's your garden variety, versatile **spade**. This will perform a wide range of tasks; from moving compost around the yard, to harvesting your first crop of potatoes, to digging holes for planting your fruit or nut trees.

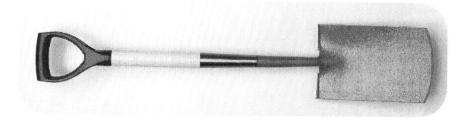

You'll also need a good quality **garden fork**. This will come in handy for turning over your gorgeous compost and a heap of other tasks.

A **rake** is a necessity when it comes time to give your planting area a level surface with a nice tilth for your seeds to go in.

There are such a wide range of **hoes** available in all sorts of shapes and sizes, but essentially a hoe is a blade on a stick. You'll need it to weed around your plants, so I prefer one with a smaller blade, so that I'm not disturbing the tender roots of my young plants.

If you can only afford to pay for one thing of real quality, make it your **secateurs**. They will last a very long time if you treat them with respect and they are an essential part of gardening maintenance.

The other things you will also need straight away are a hand trowel, hose and / or irrigation system, labels and a 2B pencil.

Most other tools you can buy as you go, or as you discover a need for a particular tool. You can improvise with things from the kitchen or shed until money allows you to go and get something designed for the job.

Create a Small 'No – Dig', Raised Plot

*T*his method of vegetable gardening is what I prefer. As you might have guessed, it doesn't involve digging. This method is particularly suited to older people or people with physical disabilities. But I just prefer it because I think it's better for the soil and easier to manage.

When soil is turned over it destroys the soil structure. When you create a no-dig plot you are not disturbing the topsoil at all. This means that the soil microbes, worms and other creatures can continue doing what they do best in your garden.

For the best results in your garden, you want to aim for no compaction of the soil as well. Water, air and nutrients travel through the soil by pathways made by worms and plant roots. When soil is compacted these pathways are destroyed.

I don't even walk on my veggie beds. By designing your plots to be no more than say 1.25metres (4 feet) across (and however long you want) you can avoid having to stand in it. You should be able to reach in from both sides to do your planting, mulching, fertilizing and harvesting.

If you start with a small bed, (say 1.25m x 2.5m / 4' x 8') you can plan it so that you can expand when you are ready.

No matter what your location, no dig vegetable gardens are a great option. It means that it doesn't matter what sort of soil you are starting out with as the layering of materials over the surface will continue to feed and condition your soil.

Eventually you will end up with dark, nutrient-rich soil.

A No Dig garden bed is made on top of the ground. It can be built over existing garden beds, lawns and even hard or rocky ground – even concrete. It should be situated in an area that receives at least six hours sun (preferably morning sun) a day and that has good drainage.

When preparing the plot it is not necessary to pull up lawn or an existing garden, you will be 'smothering' what is already there.

Building your plot

I like to install irrigation before building my plot as I find it saves me so much time and trickle irrigation (on a timer) is a far better way to water than by hand or sprinkler.

One thing to always remember when handling manures, soil or any organic matter is to always wear tough gloves to protect you from bacteria getting into any cuts. Then wash your hands thoroughly when you're finished in the garden.

1. Form the outside walls of your plot. You can use logs, old planks (make sure they haven't been treated), pavers, bricks, stones, sleepers etc. If you have disabilities you may need to get help with this.

2. Lay down a thick layer of wet newspaper (I use an old baby bath filled with water to soak the newspaper), making sure it

completely covers the enclosed area. It should be at least 6mm (quarter inch) thick and overlap by about 75mm (3inches). This will kill off any weeds or grass and prevent more from growing. Only use newspaper as glossy, coloured paper has chemicals.

3. Lay down pads (or biscuits) of lucerne hay or pea straw, making sure there are no gaps between the pads.

4. Add a 20mm (¾inch) layer of good organic fertilizer (mature chicken manure is great).

5. Cover with about 200mm (8inches) thick of loose straw.

6. Add another 20mm (¾inch) layer of good organic fertilizer (blood & bone etc).

7. Finish off with a top layer of compost, about 100mm (4inches) thick.

8. Water well and allow to settle.

9. Plant out seedlings after 2 or 3 weeks (not seeds).

Some of the benefits of creating a no-dig, raised plot include:

- can be built anywhere, any time to any design
- keeping your garden tidy, with easy access
- stops birds from scratching your mulch everywhere
- it mirrors nature by creating a rich, organic environment for your plants
- once set up, it's virtually maintenance free
- helps prevent destruction from snails, rabbits etc.

In your new raised garden bed the best veggies to start with are potatoes, lettuce, brassicas (cabbage / cauliflower family) and cucurbits (cucumber family), depending on the time of year. Root crops are better after a few seasons, when your plot has matured.

It is better to have mixed plantings of vegetables and herbs, rather than long rows or a whole bed of one type of plant. Companion Planting

(www.1stoporganicgardening.com/cp1.htm) benefits your garden in many ways, including pest and disease prevention and growing healthier, more vigorous plants.

Keeping your beds topped up with compost and / or mulch helps prevent weeds, retain moisture and nourishes your plants, promoting steady healthy growth.

This is how my plot started – very humble beginnings. Just to quickly recap; no digging, just build a structure and start adding the good stuff.

This photo was taken on September 2nd.

This is the very same plot just 10 weeks later – photo taken on November 11th.

We're already enjoying some vegetables on our dinner plates.

Growing Your Food From Seeds

*P*ropagating plants from seed is what nature does all the time. Most seeds have certain **basic requirements to germinate successfully** – the right amount of moisture, warmth, air and light, although most will germinate in the light or dark.

Larger seeds can usually be successfully sown outside, directly in your garden beds, but for the rest you can give them the best start by sowing them under glass or in seedling trays or pots. Once seeds have germinated, light is essential for healthy growth.

You need to have an idea of **the best time of year** to sow particular seeds for your area. Talk to other gardeners nearby, friends and family. If your area suffers from frosts throughout winter it is best to leave sowing your spring / summer vegetables until the last of the frosts. Use the charts at the end of this book as a general guide.

Of course if you have a glasshouse or a sunny spot inside you can get a bit of a head start. Some plants are meant to be grown through the winter, such as most peas and beans, onions, many root crops – and others will cope through milder winters, so your location is very relevant.

All in all, growing your own food and saving the seed is a very rewarding pastime. I must emphasise again that good record keeping is essential in all aspects of organic gardening, but especially for seed collection and saving.

Your garden diary and the seeds you save can become a great legacy to leave for your children – along with the love of gardening and giving your body healthy fuel.

I developed my love of gardening from watching my grandpa in his garden. He truly loved to spend time in it. It would have been wonderful if he had kept a journal of some kind. But he did save seeds, which I was given when he passed over. Those memories, along with his saved seed encouraged me to create my own organic garden.

I encourage you to get growing with your own seed, your neighbour's seed, seed from anyone who's willing to share, or even purchased seed.

See page 84 for Vegetable Sowing Chart for Southern Hemisphere.

See page 86 for Vegetable Sowing Chart for Northern Hemisphere.

Transplanting Your Seedlings Successfully

*T*ransplanting seedlings is one of my favourite tasks in the garden. There are a few simple things to consider to give your young plants the best chance to flourish – and you want them to thrive, rather than just survive.

Timing

Think about the time of year. Just because certain seedlings are available at your nursery, don't assume it's the right time to plant them out. If you're not sure, read the label – most tell you the best time of year to plant. You could look in gardening books, research online or ask family or friends who are gardeners (they might even give you some seedlings if they've bought too many) and there's a seed planting chart at the end of this book.

You can plant tender plants before the risk of late frosts has passed, provided you listen closely to weather forecasts and are prepared to cover your 'babies' with protection or enclose them in a cloche.

Hardening Off

If you've grown your seedlings from seed before you probably know to harden them off before planting. But if you're buying them from a nursery take a look at where they've been living. Have they been in a glass-house, under shade or exposed to the weather? If you seedlings have been grown outside exposed to the weather, they won't need hardening off. But if they've been pampered, they'll need a bit of toughening up to prepare them for the real world.

To harden off your seedlings you need to leave them outdoors for a longer stretch of time each day. Protect them under a porch or behind shade-cloth, bringing them indoors at night for the first few days. After a couple of days, you can expose them to the morning sun. At the end of a week, they'll be tough enough to transplant to their permanent plot.

Planting Out

The garden bed they are being planted in should already have been prepared with layers of organic matter, compost and mulch.

Always water your seedlings 10 - 30 minutes before planting out.

Before removing seedlings from their containers, arrange them where they will be planted. When you're happy with the arrangement, use a trowel to dig a hole about twice the size of the rootball. Doing this prep work reduces the length of time that the roots will be exposed (drying out).

Fill each hole with water. This supplies moisture to the plant's root zone rather than the surface where it may quickly evaporate. Gently ease the first plant from its container, working from the bottom and sides to loosen it.

Don't try and pull your seedling from the container by its stem – you may damage it. Only handle these young plants by their individual leaves or by the root ball. Keeping the rootball intact will help prevent transplant stress, so gently tease the roots to loosen them if necessary.

Place the plant into the ground at about the same level that it was growing in it's container. Backfill the hole until it is almost level with the soil. I like to add some organic fertilizer at this stage, to give my 'babies' a head start. Just use a small amount – you can add more later.

Finish backfilling, pressing the soil lightly around the roots to ensure good soil-to-root contact.

Water them in well, avoiding overhead watering, immediately after transplanting. Water daily for about a week until seedlings are well established. Bring mulch around the plant, leaving about a 10cm (4inch) diameter clear around each plant.

Other things to consider

Avoid transplanting vegetable seedlings when the weather is expected to be excessively hot. If you can, choose a day that is cloudy or transplant late in the afternoon or evening so that your plants can recover through the cool of the night, without sunlight beating down on them. If you can't do this it's a good idea to provide some temporary shade, particularly in hot weather.

An initial watering with an organic seaweed fertilizer will provide a wide range of nutrients and help reduce stress on your young seedlings.

Get all of your equipment ready before you start – hand trowel, gardening gloves, kneeling pad, your water bottle and hat.

Tomatoes are an exception to the rule as far as planting depth goes. You can plant them right down to the first set of true leaves. They will grow new roots right up to the soil level, making them more sturdy.

Seedlings from the Cucumber family (cucumbers, squash, pumpkins, melons) do better planted in hills. This allows for better drainage and warms their soil to give them a better start.

Enrich your soil.

Before you reach for your spade, consider if you have chosen the best position for your plant – does the spot you've chosen have enough shade or sun for that particular plant? Have you allowed enough room to accommodate the height and width of the plant when it is mature?

If you have poor soil where you intend to place your lovingly selected plant, you'll give it the best chance of thriving by improving the soil before planting. You can do this by making several successive applications of organic matter to the soil around where you are planting.

You can use compost, well aged animal manures, lucerne hay, worm castings etc. Apply each layer to the soil surface, about 10cm (4inches) deep. **Don't dig it in** – worms and soil microbes willingly take on this task for you. It will take a while and several applications over a few months for your soil condition to show improvement, but it will happen!

When you're ready to plant, dig the hole about double the width of the pot, but only slightly deeper. Loosen the soil in the bottom of the hole and score the sides of the hole with your garden fork. Push a little of the soil back into the hole and settle your plant onto it, making sure that it is no deeper or higher in the ground than it was in the pot. If the plant was a little pot-bound, tease the roots and spread them out over the mound of soil in the hole, removing any damaged roots with a sharp pair of secateurs.

Gently back-fill the hole around the plant and water in well.

Cover the soil surface around the plant with a 10 cm (4inch) layer of mulch, such as wood-chip, compost, pea straw or well rotted manure. Your plant should quickly adapt to its new home.

Don't add compost to planting holes.

We are often advised to add generous amounts of compost in the planting hole. I recommend against this for several reasons. For one, it can be particularly harmful in poorly drained soils.

The natural process is for leaves and other organic matter to fall onto the soil and break down slowly, which nourishes plants and builds up the topsoil. Filling your planting hole with a concentration of topsoil can lead to problems.

If the organic matter isn't fully composted, the composting process will continue underground, removing nutrients and oxygen from the soil, rather than enriching it. If the surrounding soil is poor, the plant's roots will not explore further than the hole it was planted in, virtually making it 'pot-bound' in the ground.

As the organic matter continues to break down it will decrease in volume, causing the plant to sink in the planting hole. If it was planted in poorly draining soil, the plant will be sitting in a 'plug' of water and most likely suffer root-rot.

Back-fill the hole with the soil you removed. Add compost or mulch to the surface and water in well.

The Best Ways To Water

My favourite way to water is to use a seepage hose. They are recycled tyres that allow the water to seep into the ground. The end has a normal hose connection so you can just connect your hose directly from the tap to your seepage hose.

I place it in a bit of a snake figure til I'm fairly sure that the entire veggie plot is covered. Then I add a layer of mulch over the hose to keep it in place and to help prevent moisture loss.

Drip irrigation can work well too, providing you make sure that the water spread reaches all of your plants.

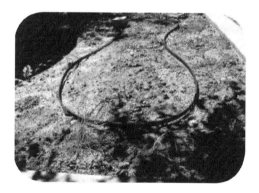

Avoid overhead 'spray' type irrigation as the plants need the water at their roots. It can lead to mildew problems and quite a lot of the water is lost to evaporation (wasteful and environmentally unsound).

If you want to get really 'high tech' you can attach a timer to your tap – just set and forget!

You'll need to thoroughly wet the soil once a week unless you are getting good rain falls. If you just sprinkle a little every day you'll just be wetting the surface. This tends to encourage shallow root growth.

You want to encourage deep root development. Your plants are less likely to suffer water stress when you water deeply. That's why you need to water deeply – once a week, or more often during hot, dry summers. Drip, trickle or soakage irrigation are the best ways to encourage deep roots and water conservation.

You will find that the more you use organic soil conditioners, fertilizers and mulches, the faster your soil will improve and will be able to retain moisture longer. Make sure that you are aware of, and abide by, any local water restrictions.

This is the same plot once it has been covered with pea straw mulch. I also put a couple of rubber snakes out and move them regularly to deter the blackbirds from getting in the mulch and scratching it about. This works if you move the snakes every day.

You'll also notice that I have a large rainwater tank right next to the plot. The rainwater is collected directly from my carport. If you want to use this idea, you might need to invest in a small pump as the water pressure is quite low.

Mulching Is A Must!

The word "mulch" comes from the old English word "melsc" – meaning rotten hay. In today's language it has come to mean any material that covers the soil to preserve moisture content, prevent soil erosion and inhibit weed growth. For organic gardening I choose materials that will break down over time, feeding my plants and contributing to the amount of humus in the soil.

Many materials are suitable to use as mulch, such as: leaves, pine needles, straw / hay, sawdust, gravel / rocks, paper / cardboard, grass clippings, carpet underfelt and even plastic. Each one has its own benefits and disadvantages.

Dark mulches warm the soil, whereas light coloured mulches will keep the soil cooler. In a cool climate light-coloured straw mulch will hold back the development of many hot season vegetables – so take care with your choice of mulch and the time of year you apply it.

I've heard it said that mulches can be a refuge for problem garden pests, but nature balances this with enough predators to consume any rise in pest numbers.

Leaves are the most natural mulch of all. However most of the nutritional content has been taken from the tree before the leaf falls to the ground. Many leaves contain tannins and some have growth suppressants (eucalypts & pine needles for example), so it's better to either add them to your compost heap or place them in a wire container and allow them to decompose for a year or so and become leaf mould, then use as mulch.

Straw / Hay is my preferred method of mulching in my organic food garden. The main advantage over many mulches is that it slowly releases nutrients to feed the plants it surrounds.

One disadvantage is that hay may contain weed seeds, but they are usually very easy to pull. That is why I prefer pea straw – usually the only weeds are peas and they add nitrogen to the soil. Another problem can be that it may become water repellent. But this is not a problem if you trickle or flood irrigate your food plots.

Sawdust is probably best used by composting it before laying as a mulch as it may rob the soil of nitrogen, especially if your soil is poor to begin with. Also, it can become water repellent. However if you have a good supply it makes an excellent soft, natural looking covering for pathways.

Gravel / Rocks are best used outside of your veggie garden unless you live in a cool climate area and use them around warm climate plants, such as pumpkins and tomatoes. Rocks store heat from the sun during the day and slowly release it through the night.

They can also be used in arid areas around larger plants and trees. Water condenses on the underside of the rocks as they cool during the night helping to keep plants moist.

The disadvantage with rocks is that weeds will grow around them.

Paper / Cardboard are both quite useful as mulches. I often use thick layers of newspaper (which I wet before laying) underneath pea-straw or pine bark. The layers need to overlap about 15cm to prevent weeds from coming through. Don't use pages with coloured ink as they may contain heavy metals.

Cardboard can make a great mulch under young trees. You can secure it with rocks in a decorative way in addition to straw or bark. Using cardboard beneath sawdust for your garden paths will prevent most weeds.

Grass clippings can be utilised as a thin mulch under trees and shrubs that will feed your plants as it breaks down. Take care not to pile on too thickly though as you will end up with a water repelling, smelly blob!

Carpet underfelt makes an excellent mulch in your organic garden. It won't blow away, it's easy to cut to insert your seedlings, it allows air to penetrate and it holds moisture very well. You must make sure that it is the older underfelt though, not the modern foam type.

Black plastic has the advantage of being cheap, easy to install and a great weed suppressor, but its disadvantages are many. It doesn't feed the soil, it deteriorates with direct sunlight and doesn't allow the natural gas exchanges between the air and soil.

Whatever your choice of mulch, your garden will be more productive and well balanced if you choose a feeding kind of mulch. Remember too that mulches should not come into contact with the stems of you plants as this may cause them to rot.

Keeping On Top Of Weeds

$t\ell$'m sure we've all heard the old saying that weeds really are just plants growing where you don't want them to. Unwanted volunteers (or weeds) can be easily controlled with just a few minutes each week. A hoe makes shallow cultivation very easy, without disturbing your precious vegetables.

Weeds are quite easy to pull when they're small, especially if they've grown through thick mulch – plus they are far less likely to germinate under thick mulch in the first place. So that's my number 1 tip – always mulch heavily!

Some other ways to quickly get rid of weeds are:

- Build a compost heap over them – the heap will heat up and everything underneath will "cook". Move it to the next patch when it has matured and grow vegetables where the original heap was.
- If you have a larger area, build a raised bed over the area. Fill it with layers of good soil, compost and mulch. Any weeds that manage to survive this treatment and poke through the top will be easy to remove.
- Grow a patch of potatoes over them – they end up smothering out other plants when heavily mulched.

BUT, it's not always such a bad thing having some weeds in your garden. "WHAT?" I hear you scream. Well it's true. There are a number of benefits for having weeds in your garden.

Firstly, many weeds **attract beneficial insects** – that is insects that prey on pests that might be causing problems in your garden. Some weed flowers are a food source for insects such as hoverflies, bees and wasps. These beneficial insects eat aphids and other pests. Can you see how it could be a good thing to have them on your team? Besides, it's always easier to work with Mother Nature, than against her. And after all, that is the premise of organic gardening.

Secondly, if you do some research you will find that many plants that may now be considered weeds, were once considered food. These include dandelion, horseradish, nettles – and yes, they are still quite edible. My mother makes a great veggie soup, and with the addition of nettles means it will be rich in iron.

And thirdly, some weeds are really deep-rooted. They excel at mining minerals from deep down in the soil, which are then stored in their leaves. You can use their leaves in your compost heap, where the minerals will then be released and made available to your vegetables as you add the compost to them.

Deep-rooted plants also help break up heavy soils, leaving tunnels when the plant dies and breaks down, for air and water to penetrate deeply.

You can either harvest their leaves by hand or you can mow them and then add them to your compost heap.

If you keep harvesting the leaves and don't allow the "weed" to go to seed, you will eventually weaken them over the years and they will die. You just have to be vigilant and not allow the weeds to flower and produce seeds.

How To Make Your Own Liquid Fertilizers

$\mathcal{W}$e all need a bit of a "pick-me-up" from time to time and your vegetables, herbs, fruits and soil will also benefit from a boost of liquid tonic every now and then. It's not a good idea to force your plants to feed when they drink, so I don't recommend regular weekly feeding, but just as a boost.

We all want the best results from our efforts in the garden. Giving your veggies a liquid boost can provide them with nutrients and trace elements that are not always available to them.

Making your own liquid fertilizer is a simple task that can be done in just a few minutes. Then it's just a matter of waiting for it to mature, which can take up to a month.

The basic equipment you need is a large plastic container with a tightly fitting lid. The container must never have been used for toxic chemicals.

Make different brews, depending on what you're wanting to accomplish. When it has matured, dilute to a pale yellow colour, otherwise it may be too strong. Then use as you need it, both on the soil and /or as a foliage spray.

Weeds

Often if you have a particular weed problem in your garden, it is there to help restore the balance of nutrients in the soil. If you make a liquid manure from that particular weed and use it as a foliar spray, it will often reduce the recurrence of that weed.

Also, deep-rooted weeds such as dandelion, dock, yarrow, burnet and wire-weed bring nutrients to the surface that have leached down into the sub-soil.

Nettle 'Tea'

A brew made from stinging nettles (Urtica) will encourage growth in spring. Use gloves when pulling up the nettles. You need to fill your container with nettles and completely cover with water. Allow the mix to ferment until the nettles have completely broken down.

Fish

Place fish scraps in your container and just cover with water. Make sure you have a tight fitting lid to prevent flies getting to it (and the smell from getting to you). Let it ferment for about a month. It should be mostly decomposed by then. This brew is a rich source of trace elements, so you need to use it very diluted.

Comfrey

If you want to give your fruiting plants, such as pumpkins and tomatoes a boost, try a liquid manure made from comfrey as it is very high in potash. It will break down quickly and with very little solid residue as its leaves contain a high amount of water.

Compost

If you need a fungal preventative, make a tea from compost. The compost must have some animal manure included for this to work. Put some compost in a hessian bag and soak in water for a few days. You'll need to dilute it to the colour of weak tea, then spray on plant leaves every 10 – 14 days.

Natural Insect, Pest & Disease Control

*O*rganic gardeners always prefer to use methods that have the least negative effect on the environment. By growing strong healthy plants we eliminate the threat of having large scale pest invasions.

But when some pest populations do build up in our garden we should be asking **"how can I encourage more predators?"**, rather than "what should I do about all these pests?"

For every pest you have in excess there is at least one, and probably many predators that would happily relieve you of the excess. Sometimes it takes predator populations a little longer to build than it does the pest it feasts on, so give it a little time before pulling out the big guns – insecticides.

Remember that 'organic' does not mean less poisonous and that most sprays are indiscriminate and really should only be used as a last resort. Bearing that in mind, here are some organic ways to deal with a few persistent bug problems.

Bug Juice – A very effective insecticide. Sounds a bit disgusting, but worth trying if you can stomach it!

Collect an assortment of pests – grasshoppers are excellent – from wherever you are having pest problems in your garden.

Liquefy them in a blender with the addition of one part water to about two parts in volume of bugs. Strain and dilute to about 5ml of bug juice per 1litre of water. Spray on affected plants.

Snails and Slugs

Fortunately there are a few easy ways to deal with these ravenous creatures as they can devour your tender seedlings overnight.

Ducks are great snail and slug hunters and will delight wandering around the garden in search and destroy mode. The only minor damage you can expect is from their heavy feed, but they'll generally not eat your greens like chickens would.

Of course you can collect the snails and slugs and throw them to your chickens if you keep them – they'll be delighted! The best time for collection is dawn and dusk when it is moist. You can also make this job easier by having cardboard or similar on the ground where they will gather.

If you don't have chickens or ducks another method is similar to the bug juice above. You need to gather some snails and/or slugs into a container with some added sugar and water. Allow it to ferment for a few days then place in the blender. You can dilute it further with water if you don't have much 'juice' and sprinkle it around problem areas.

Another method is to make a **coffee spray**. This works by spraying it thoroughly on and around the seedlings you want to protect. When the snails or slugs cross areas that have been sprayed they absorb the caffeine and die.

Dilute one part strong espresso coffee to 10 parts hot water. When it's cool, pour into a spray bottle and spray on plants that you want to protect and the immediate area around them.

Then there's the time honoured traditional snail catcher – yes, the old **beer in the jar trap**. Partly fill a jar with beer (stale of course, you don't want to waste the good stuff) and lay it on its side where they are most active. They are attracted to the beer, get drunk and die. What a way to go!

An alternative to this is vegemite dissolved in water. They are attracted to the yeast.

Mealy bugs look like white, fluffy slaters. They are sap-sucking insects that cause leaves to wilt and go yellow. You may find them feasting away on your fruiting plants and ornamentals such as palms, ferns, orchids and succulents.

They prefer the sheltered conditions of a glass house or indoors. Mealy bugs exude a sweet, sticky substance called honeydew which can lead to sooty mould fungus and ants (ants feed on the honeydew).

The best way to deal with them is to prune off the most damaged parts of the plant and then kill any remaining bugs by dabbing them with a cottonwool ball dipped in methylated spirits. This will dissolve their waxy protective coating, they will dehydrate and die.

Scale are also sucking insects that feed on plant sap. They form in thick clusters on the leaves and soft growth of many garden plants. They also produce honeydew as a waste by-product of their feeding. Heavy infestations can cause stunted growth and wilting.

If you only have a small infestation you can scrape them off your plant with your fingernail or a toothbrush. Larger numbers can be sprayed with a solution of homemade oil spray.

You can also use the oil spray to eliminate citrus leaf-miner and red spider mite. When you coat them thoroughly, the pests are suffocated by the oil.

Home-made oil spray.

1. Add 500ml of vegetable oil to 250ml of pure liquid soap to a bowl.
2. Mix together in a blender and then store in a jar.
3. Dilute 1tablespoon in 1litre of water. Spray, making sure you get under all the leaves.

Special Note: Have kitchen utensils and a blender that are dedicated specifically for the purpose of spray preparation.

Use all sprays with extreme caution and do not eat from any plant that has been sprayed <u>for at least two weeks.</u>

Controlling insects and pests naturally can sometimes be difficult. Here are some of the best ways to help reduce your losses without resorting to harmful chemicals.

➢ Choose disease resistant varieties
➢ Discard sickly looking seedlings
➢ Keep your plants growing vigorously
➢ Clean up crop waste as quickly as practical
➢ Keep out weeds which encourage insects and disease
➢ Hand-pick insects like caterpillars, hose off aphids
➢ Water at soil level, so plants are not wet at night
➢ Dispose of any diseased plants before they contaminate others
➢ Don't throw diseased plants in your compost heap
➢ Rotate your garden beds / plots
➢ Encourage natural predators wherever possible
➢ Insect traps can work for snails and slugs
➢ Learn about companion planting methods

Deterring Pest Birds

Blackbirds are a real pest in my veggie garden here in the Barossa Valley, South Australia. They look for insects and grubs on the ground with their feet and beaks by pushing around mulch and leaf-litter.

This really annoys me when I've just laid out a fresh layer of mulch because they make such a mess and sometimes end up burying or damaging my plants. So I tried a little experiment with several rubber snakes around my veggie plots to see if it makes a difference. Guess what? It actually works, provided I move the snakes to different positions each day. Remove their nests if you find them under your eaves or verandas, to discourage them breeding around your property. They build medium to large fibre and mud nests.

Easy To Grow Vegetables

*W*hen you're just starting out as a newcomer to organic gardening, it's great to get some successes on the board as soon as possible. I've put this list together of **my top 10 easiest veggies to grow** to encourage you to get started. Once you discover how easy it is to grow your own delicious, healthy veggies, you'll be scratching your head wondering why you didn't try it sooner.

So start out with these, then when you've had success you can research other veggies, fruits and nuts that you want to try. Always bear in mind the climate zone you live in and when the plants like to grow, so that you are working with Mother Nature.

Radish

Radishes are probably the easiest vegetable to start out with. They thrive in all climates, all year round in temperate zones. The other great thing about them is that they mature really quickly, from seed to eating in as little as 4 or 5 weeks.

They rarely have any pest or disease problems because they grow so quickly.

If you've already enriched the soil with organic compost all you need do is keep the water up to them, especially in hot, dry weather – mulch in summer, but not in winter. If you've used plenty of seed you may need to thin them as they get bigger. Pick them as soon as they're a reasonable size or they become woody.

Silverbeet, Spinach or Swiss Chard

This group of vegetables are related and are also quite easy to grow. Spinach grows best in cooler climates, but silverbeet will grow all year round in temperate zones.

If you're growing them from seed, soak them overnight. Sow seeds about 30cm (12 inches) apart by placing them on the soil surface and poking with your finger to the depth of about 1cm (half inch). Cover with soil and water in well.

Keep them well watered in hot weather and apply organic fertilizer every month, giving them an occasional feed with an organic liquid fertilizer. Mulching with compost or pea-straw will help conserve water, control weeds and feed your soil.

When the leaves are big enough to use, pick from the outside making sure you leave at least 5 or 6 stalks in the centre for the plant to continue growing.

Capsicum (peppers) and Chillies

These plants are also related to each other and enjoy the same growing conditions. They are a warm climate vegetable and will not set fruit if the overnight temperatures are too low. You can grow both capsicum and chillies in pots.

You may need to stake capsicum for wind protection if you grow them vigorously, as they can reach up to 80cm (30inches).

Sow in seed boxes in spring. When your seedlings have reached 15cm (6inches), transplant them into beds prepared with compost at about 50cm (20inches) apart.

Fertilize with organic pellets every 4 or 5 weeks when they start to flower. Make sure you don't over do it, or you will end up with very healthy plants with lots of leaves, but very little fruit.

You can harvest capsicum at any time, but if you wait for the fruit to turn red (they all start out green) they have much higher amounts of vitamin C.

Leave chillies on the plant to mature, then they can be harvested and used fresh. If you want to dry some just leave them in a dark, dry, airy place for several weeks.

They will store well in glass jars for many years. Remember never to touch your eyes after handling chillies as it is very painful. Wash your hands thoroughly.

Cherry Tomatoes

Tomatoes will grow in most soils and all but the coldest climates. And cherry tomatoes are the easiest to grow, so they suit new gardeners perfectly. They will even grow well as tub specimens. It's not essential to stake them, provided you don't mind them sprawling around the place a bit.

They are frost tender, so you can start them indoors if your area has late frosts. When your seedlings get to 15 – 20cm (6-8inches), transplant them into their permanent position, whether it be tub or ground.

If you are going to stake them, get your stakes in first so you don't damage their young root system. Tomatoes (unlike most plants) actually benefit from being planted deeper than they were in the seedling box. You can even bury the bottom leaves. This actually benefits the plant as they grow roots right up to the soil surface, giving it more stability and accessibility to water and nutrients.

If growing them in the ground, give them at least 50cm (20inches) spacing.

Deep water you plants regularly and give a thick layer of mulch.

Providing you're planting your tomatoes in a compost-rich soil, you will only need to liquid fertilize when fruiting starts. Use a good organic liquid manure such as Seasol or Maxicrop and use as a foliar spray.

Pick your tomatoes as they ripen, to encourage more fruit.

Zucchini

You will find zucchini one of the easiest vegetables to grow, with amazing yields. They just keep giving! Zucchini are part of the cucumber / melon / pumpkin family and enjoy a warm growing season.

Sow 2 or 3 seeds directly into a mound of richly composted soil in late spring, or after frosts are over. You can train zucchini to grow up a trellis or fence, which can help prevent powdery mildew. When the seedlings are about 10cm (4inches) tall, gently pull out all but the strongest plant.

You'll need about 3 or 4 mounds (plants) to feed a family of 4 – 6. Give them plenty of water and add organic fertilizer every 4 weeks or so. When the zucchini reach between 15 and 20 cm (6-8inches) it's time to pick them.

They can grow really quickly – literally overnight – so keep a vigilant eye on them otherwise you'll end up with inedible veggies. You also want to pick them as they're ready to keep the yields high.

Butternut Pumpkins

Pumpkins are known for being easy to grow. Belonging to the same family as zucchini, they grow in similar conditions. Again plant seeds in mounds and keep the strongest seedling. Have your mounds about a metre (yard) apart.

Mulch around the mound and keep the water up to them in really hot and dry weather. Feed every 3 weeks with well rotten manure or mature compost.

Here's where the difference comes in. You need to leave pumpkins on the vine to fully mature. Wait until the vines have died off before harvesting (somewhere between 14 & 20 weeks).

Before any chance of frost, harvest by cutting the stems at least 5cm (2inches) from the pumpkin.

Store in a dry place until needed.

Leeks and Spring Onions

Spring onions and leeks are in the Allium family and grow in very similar conditions. You can grow in seed raising mix or seed directly where they are to grow. If you grow seeds in punnets you can transplant seedlings when they are about 20cm (8inches) tall into well prepared beds (they like a little lime if your soil is acidic), about 20cm apart.

Some people like to "blanch" the stems of leeks to keep them white, but I don't bother. All you really need to do for leeks and spring onions is give them plenty of water, mulch to keep the weeds down and the soil moist and apply organic fertilizer every few weeks.

Harvest when leeks are about 2cm (an inch) thick, and spring onions as they become big enough.

Bush or Dwarf Beans

There are many different varieties of beans to choose from. When you're starting out, go for the bush or dwarf varieties. Grow these beans in warm weather as beans don't like the cold (unless you're growing broad beans – different story).

Fertilize along the row where your beans are to grow. Don't let your bean seeds come into direct contact with your organic fertilizer. Sow your beans directly where they are to grow, into damp soil and avoid watering near them for the first few days. (Don't soak seeds before planting).

Space rows at 60cm (24inches) and push seeds about 2cm (an inch) into the soil, 10cm (4inches) apart. A row about 3 or 4 metres (yards) long should be enough for a family of 5.

To get a continuous supply of beans, start your next sowing when the first crop has grown their first true leaves. Feed with a liquid organic fertilizer when flowering starts. Remember to harvest your beans while they're young and tender. They taste better this way, but more importantly, they will give you much better yields.

If you want to save your own seeds, leave the healthiest pods on the bush until they have completely dried. Then pick and pod them, storing in a dry place until next season. Remember to label them.

Peas

Peas will yield heavily if you give them what they need. And they are so delicious! Most varieties love the same conditions. Plant in late summer through to late winter, providing your soil is still workable. Peas like a higher pH than most vegetables, so add some lime into the soil along with mature compost or organic fertilizer.

Provide support by giving them something to climb up. Plant seeds every 5cm (2inches) in a well-drained soil with a sunny position and provide support with small sticks or similar until they reach what you want to grow them on.

Keep down any weeds with good organic mulch. Feed with an organic liquid fertilizer every 3 or 4 weeks. Keep moist in dry weather. Pick regularly to increase yields. Save seed the same as you would beans.

Beetroot

I love growing beetroot. It's so easy to grow – but let me say this up front; it's quite different from the tinned supermarket kind.

Plant throughout spring and summer. Add lime to your soil a couple of weeks before planting if your soil is a bit acid. Take your seeds and soak them overnight. Sow directly in the soil, about 1cm (half inch) deep and 30cm (12inches) apart. Cover lightly with soil and water them in.

If you want a continuous supply, plant your next crop every 2 – 3 weeks.

At about 4 or 5 weeks, give them a feed with organic liquid fertilizer.

You pull your beets when they have grown to about 6 to 8 cm (2 to 3 inches) in diameter, roughly 8 to 10 weeks after planting. Don't leave them to grow huge as they just become tough and woody.

The young leaves are great in a salad. I love to roast or boil them. They make great juice when added to apple and carrot. I've also pickled them and turned them into soup – very unusual, but delicious.

So there you have it – the 10 easiest veggies to grow. If you're short on garden space you can try growing some of these in pots. You just need to remember to make sure you water when needed.

I wish you every success in getting started gardening organically. If you already garden, have a go at getting your kids (or grandkids) to try growing these veggies themselves. You'll be surprised at how much more eager they are to eat something they've grown themselves.

*H*erbs are such a wonderful gift from mother nature in so many ways. Their uses are many, including culinary; medicinal; household; cosmetic and craft. Not to mention their uses in the garden as companion plants and many can be used as activators in the compost heap.

And there's no better way to delight in their pungent aromatic qualities than to grow them right outside your kitchen door.

Once you have a herb garden you will fall in love with them. Most herbs are fairly easy to grow. They don't have to take up much space, or much of your time.

Thyme

Herbs don't suffer much from insect attack and they are not prone to disease problems. Most will survive even if quite neglected – but we want our herbs to grow healthy and vigorously to best serve us. So let's look at creating the best conditions for your herb garden.

Where To Grow Your Herbs

If you are lucky enough to have plenty of room for a plot dedicated to growing herbs, then that's great. A creative and practical way to grow herbs together is in a spiral. I like to interplant herbs throughout my garden, taking advantage of their wonderful companion planting benefits, as well as having the ones I use most in the kitchen close by for easy access.

Many herbs originate from the Mediterranean and prefer conditions suited to that climate. Such as hot, dry summers and cool, wet winters. Often the hotter the summer, the more aromatic the oils of the herb become.

Although most herbs will grow in partial shade, they will grow best if you choose a site with between 4 and 6 hours of sunlight per day.

The majority of herbs prefer a well-drained soil, but will cope with varying soil types. You can always improve your starting soil by adding organic matter, including compost and mulching. If your soil doesn't drain well you might consider building raised beds or growing your herbs in containers.

Most herbs don't require much in the way of fertilizers. Adding compost as a mulch with a layer of pea straw or similar over the top is enough to keep most herbs thriving.

Growing Your Herbs In Containers

Herbs are some of the easiest plants to grow in containers. With some thought to position of the sun, you can grow them quite successfully on patios, balconies, terraces and verandas. This way you can quite literally have them at your back door – or even in your window sill.

Container growing is particularly useful if you live in a very cold winter climate, so that you can over-winter your herbs in containers indoors.

It's also a great way to grow some of the herbs you use regularly if you're renting. When you leave you just take your herb containers with you!

You can choose pretty much any container to grow herbs in. You could get quite creative with your container as long as it has enough drainage and is not something that may have any toxic residue. But if you're not all that creative there are custom planters, large shallow pots that allow several types of herbs to grow together, strawberry pots and window boxes – and I'm sure there are many more options to choose from.

Smaller herbs are going to be the best choice for container plants. You might be surprised at how many types of herbs would be happy growing together in the same pot.

Choosing slow growing herbs will mean that you won't have to keep them tidy. Snipping what you want for dinner will keep them compact and bushy. Always select healthy herbs to give them the best start. Remove any dead or diseased leaves to keep them healthy.

When potting them up into their container remember that they'll be there for a while, so choose a good, well drained potting mix. Because most herbs don't need a lot of fertilizer, choose a potting mix without added fertilizer. Container plants require more attention to watering needs as they will dry out much faster than plants in the ground. On hot, dry days you may need to water small containers twice a day.

Seasonal Care

Keeping weeds out of your herb garden and watering well during summer are the two main requirements to keeping your established herbs healthy. Mulching will be a big help with both of these tasks. This will also help keep your herb roots cool. Apply a thick layer of mulch – about 3 or 4 inches / 8-10 cm to be effective. If you live in an area with severe winters you will need to over-winter some herbs or treat them as annuals and plant new plants in spring.

Golden Oregano

If some of your herb plants start to get "leggy" trim them almost back to ground level at the end of summer. Herbs that will benefit from this include: oregano, marjoram, all the mints, yarrow, lemon balm.

Some of the more shrub-like herbs just need trimming back to encourage bushy growth, such as rosemary, lemon verbena and lavender.

And some herbs should be treated as annuals – in other words pull them up after the main growing season and plant fresh plants next growing season. These include basil, dill, chervil, borage, coriander, cumin.

You will benefit greatly by including herbs in your organic garden. They offer so much, yet ask so little.

Some herbs are best treated as groundcovers, some make delightful edging plants, but I prefer to grow most of my herbs amongst other plants. They truly come into their own when their beauty and aromas can be experienced intimately and often.

*A*ll organic gardeners love the time of year when the last frosts have been, the soil is warming up and the daffodils nod their heads, saying that spring is here. It's time to start planting your annual vegetable garden.

But what a fantastic supplement to the garden would it be if there were vegetables available that don't need to be replanted each year? You plant them once, then feed and water them and you can just keep picking them year after year.

Well, there are vegetables that you plant in a permanent position and they provide you with food on an ongoing basis. A perennial is defined as having a life cycle lasting more that two years. They generally die back during the cold winter months and emerge the following spring.

So a perennial vegetable is an edible plant that comes back each year. This way you have less to do, you disturb the soil less and your perennials become more drought and frost hardy as their roots grow deeper every year.

Soil Preparation For Perennials

All perennials will benefit from soil preparation that increases the nutrient levels and the moisture holding capacity of their garden bed. I like to grow my perennial vegetables separate from the annual plots, so that I'm not disturbing them on a regular basis.

If you have clay or heavy soils your perennials will benefit greatly if you use raised beds, as most perennials need good drainage to perform well.

Adding humus or compost to the soil will greatly improve growing conditions in heavy soils that dry out in summer, as well as lighter soils. Improving the soil will also increase the life and productivity of your perennial plants.

You want to prepare the beds well in advance of buying your plants. You want to make all of your amendments long before you bring your perennials home.

When you have got your new plants home, this is how you need to plant them into their permanent positions.

- Dig a hole in the soil twice the depth of your plant and fill with water
- Mix in a generous amount of mature, rich, organic material or compost to the soil that you took from the hole
- Backfill the hole with the humus enriched soil. The addition of the mature organic matter provides extra nutrients below the soil that will also have increased water holding capacity, maintaining the moisture available to the roots of these perennial plants throughout the dry summer months.
- Spread a light layer of organic fertiliser on top of the soil to help quickly develop a good root system

- Mulch the soil around your perennials, making sure that the mulch doesn't come right up to the crown or base of the plant as it may cause your plant to rot

Perennial Vegetables you might like to try – bearing in mind your climatic zone, as some of these perennials are not frost tolerant.

Artichokes, Asparagus, Beans (perennial), Broccoli (perennial), Cardoon, Chard (perennial), Chicory, Chives, Chokos, Corn Salad, Dandelions, Fennel, French sorrel, Garlic Chives, Ginger, Good King Henry, Japanese hornwort, Jerusalem artichokes, Lemon Balm, Lovage, New Zealand spinach, Purslane, Rhubarb, Rocket, Sorrel, Sweet potato, Tamarillo, Walking Onions.

Perennial vegetables are a perfect addition to an edible landscape gardening plan or permaculture garden. Many are very attractive and make excellent feature plants as well as give you food.

Remember that since they will grow in the same soil for many years, it is vitally important that they are given a sunny position, with well-drained soil full of organic matter. Planting perennial vegetables is a truly rewarding investment in your organic garden and you kitchen.

Each year as it warms up in spring, give your perennials a generous layer of organic fertilizer, then mulch with a layer of compost, leafmould or straw – or even better, both.

How much do I plant?

*T*his section is intended as a guide as our food needs are so varied, depending on how many there are in your family, how many meals you eat at home, how much you like to eat, how many visitors you get.

Then there's your families personal taste preferences to consider. There's not much point in growing 10 eggplant vines if only one person likes it. But if you like to make your own batch of tomato sauce to see you throughout the year, you'll want to grow extra tomatoes, onions and garlic to provide your own delicious, organic ingredients.

The following plant numbers are roughly based on the needs of a family of two adults and two children (assuming your children eat vegetables!), so add or take to suit your own requirements.

Some seasons you'll end up with an excess of some things. I've never found it to be a problem when there are so many great recipes for pickles, preserves or sauces – not to mention my friends and family who are thrilled when I turn up a box of goodies for them!

Of course you will also need to consider how much available space you have. If space is limited grow the things you like most – or vegetables that cost the most if you had to pay for them – or hard to get vegetables, that perhaps won't be particularly fresh by the time they get to your table.

Use the chart on the next page to help you decide how much to plant.

Beans	We usually grow several types – climbing and bush varieties. A seed packet in spring, then another in summer when the last lot is flowering. Grow more if you want to dry some for winter.
Beetroot	12 – 20 plants early spring, the same late spring, and again mid-summer
Broad Beans	Plant blocks of about 2 square meters late autumn / early winter. Grow more if you want to dry some
Broccoli	Twenty or so plants in mid-late summer
Brussels Sprouts	Twelve plants mid-late summer
Cabbage	12 cabbages and red cabbage in spring, plus 20 – 30 small cabbages late summer
Capsicum (peppers)	One dozen plants in spring
Carrots	Plant about a square meter per month, during spring
Cauliflower	20 – 30 plants in late summer
Celery	Around 15 plants, 30 plants if you want a lot for salads
Chilli	2 or 3 plants every other year
Corn	30 – 50 plants (in blocks) in spring, then more throughout summer

Cucumbers	6 plants in spring, then another 6 plants mid-summer
Eggplant	2 – 6 bushes
Leeks	50 – 100 plants, depending on what you use them for
Lettuce	If you eat a lot of salad 6 plants every week most of the year, except mid-winter. Plant extra late in summer for winter lettuces or grow cut & come again lettuce
Melons	6 plants or more! You can grow them among your flowers
Onions	About 400 seedlings + spring onions + chives + garlic
Parsley	A dozen flat leaf & a dozen curly leaf plants – feed well
Parsnips	Parsnip seed only germinates if it is really fresh, so you may have to sow a lot of seed your first time. But then if you let one go to seed and self-sow you'll always have enough
Peas	At least 3 packets in autumn and 3 in spring – more if you want to freeze some
Potatoes	You'll need about 200 kg a year. Plant a large sack of seed potatoes. You'll find you miss gathering some and they will produce some of your next years crop

Pumpkins	10 or 12 vines, include several bush varieties
Radish	Sow a packet of seeds every other month throughout the year
Silverbeet/Spin-ach	10 – 20 plants, a combination of Silverbeet, spin-ach & chard
Tomatoes	12 plants (double if you make sauce), 2 grafted plants, a cherry tomato, an egg tomato & a climb-ing yellow or heirloom variety
Zucchini	2 - 4 plants in spring, 2 mid-summer

How To Have More Vegetables For More Of The Year

Succession Planting is the practice of planting the same type of plant, but at timed intervals – for example a month apart. By doing this with vegetables that you use a lot, you will be able to create a much longer supply for your family.

This works best with plants that grow happily for most parts of the year; or if you're lucky enough to live in a temperate climate, even all year round.

It works like this. Say you plant lettuce at the beginning of September. You only need to grow a short row because you would plant a second row in early October; then another in early November. By the time you're planting your November succession, your September lettuce are mature enough to eat (I prefer the type where you pick and come again, rather than harvesting the whole plant). If you keep planting a row of lettuce at the start of each month, you will always have lettuce ready to pick straight from your organic garden.

You won't be subject to availability in the supermarket or price fluctuations. Now you may not need to plant that often if you don't use a great deal of lettuce. Or you could plant a similar salad crop in alternative months; perhaps rocket, or beetroot, or different varieties of lettuce. Use your own judgement to suit the needs of your family.

Some plants that work particularly well as succession plants include: lettuce, rocket, radish, spring onions, cucumbers and carrots.

Others that work well in the main growing season include: bush beans, corn, beetroot, broccoli, cabbage, silver-beet and spinach; even zucchini. Try experimenting with various vegetables that your family loves. If you end up with too much you can always give some to friends and relatives.

That brings me to another way you can be sure to get the most from your organic vegetable garden. You can increase the length of your growing season by using different varieties of the same vegetable.

For example, you can put in an early, mid-season and late variety of many vegetables. That way you'll have more of your favourite vegetables for more of the year, making whatever space you have available more productive.

You will find many fruiting plants are available in early, mid-season and late varieties too – again making it easier to provide for your family from your organic garden.

The real secret to succession (or successive) planting is planning – as with most things in the garden. Keep a garden diary or journal so you know when to put in your next crop. This will also be of great benefit in seasons to come. You won't have to rely on your memory to see what worked and what could be improved on this year. And you'll also know what you grew too much of and what you could have done with more of particular veggies.

I find it really joyful to grow my own vegetables from seed, so try saving some of your own seed too and see how you go with that.

Food Gardening In Small Spaces

*I*f you live in an apartment or only have quite limited space to grow your food plants, don't despair. There are numerous solutions to gardening in small spaces.

Space can be at a premium, especially these days when apartments and condos are so popular. A simple solution for those wanting to grow at least a few basic herbs and vegetables is to grow in containers.

Maybe you don't have the time to maintain a large vegetable garden, or you have a physical condition that prevents you bending down or using the usual gardening tools. Whatever the reason, container gardening can be a great way to produce some of your organic food needs.

You will be pleasantly surprised to learn how many plants will grow quite happily in containers, providing you give them what they need.

And in return you will get wonderful organic food, filled with life energy. I think that's one of the things I love most about organic gardening – that I can pick something that I know has grown with no chemicals and eat it within 1 – 20 minutes. It's something nutritionalists and the like don't seem to consider – the value of the life energy from that plant becomes part of your life energy when you eat it.

It's little wonder that there are so many health issues these days. People end up eating more and more processed foods that are unrecognizable from their original form. But that's a whole other topic....

While container gardening may have its limitations, there are some great benefits.

- You have the advantage of being able to bring containers indoors through the coldest part of winter, prolonging the season.
- Your pots / containers can create a focal point on a balcony or patio area, adding interest, colour or foliage.
- Planters can be made from just about any type of container that holds soil and allows adequate drainage.
- Potting mediums are easy to work with as they are the correct pH.
- Weeds are much less likely to become a problem.
- Less likely to be attacked by snails, slugs, insects or soil borne diseases.
- The tiniest space – even a windowsill can be used to produce some fresh herbs

Soil

You need to purchase premium potting mix for growing in containers. Don't be tempted to use soil from the garden in your pots as it will become compact and heavy, not allowing water to drain well. A **premium potting medium** is a must. It is lighter and so provides excellent drainage.

You will need to provide all your plants nutrients as most potting mixes do not come with organic fertilizer. Remember that more is not better when it comes to applying fertilizer. Too much fertilizer in contact with your plant's roots will burn them. Always follow the directions on packaged fertilizers. There are many organic fertilizers available to choose from so look for blends suited to the type of plant you are growing - leafy, flowering, vegetables, etc.

Container plants need watering more frequently than normal garden plants, and as a result the water leaches away fertilizers. So container grown plants benefit from liquid feeds on a regular basis throughout their growing season. You can purchase organic liquid fertilizers if you don't have room or time to make your own. Use them for foliar feeding and drenching the soil around your plants.

Watering

Because container plants are above ground the sun and wind will dry potting soils out quicker than plants grown in the ground. During summer you will need to take care that your pots do not dry out.

Water containers when the soil dries out to a depth of 1-2cm (1/2 inch). Apply water with a soft flow to be gentle on your plants and the soil. In really hot weather I usually re-water about 30 minutes after my initial watering. This is beneficial in containers as plants cannot always take up the water quickly.

It is important to make sure that your containers have adequate drainage or your plants will suffer and ultimately die if the roots are permanently sitting in water. If your containers sit on the ground, bottom holes may not drain readily.

If they are on a patio or are just off the ground, there should be no problem with bottom holes. If you're not sure, make side holes or sit the pot on up off the ground on bricks or pavers.

Pieces from an old broken clay pot or fly wire placed over the drainage holes will keep the potting mix from packing around the holes and reducing drainage, as well as keeping it in the pot.

You can add some mulch to larger pots in summer to help prevent them from drying out. I like to use pea straw.

Choosing the right plants

When you're growing in containers you will need to look for varieties that are the most suitable for growing in small areas. Many herbs make excellent container specimens. Try growing several together in one pot that like similar conditions.

As for vegetables you could start with some of the smaller vegetables such as radishes, lettuce, onions, capsicum or chillies, eggplant, short varieties of carrots, bush beans etc. Container planting is ideal to try out some companion planting techniques. You'll have better success if your plant combinations are happy ones!

You can even grow tomatoes in pots. Look for smaller varieties such as cherry tomatoes or bush tomatoes that don't require staking.

If you plant in three weekly successions you may be able to achieve continuous production of some plants, such as lettuce and radishes.

Strawberries grow well in containers, particularly hanging baskets if they are not allowed to dry out.

Location

Choose a position for you container plants where they get about six hour sun each day, preferably morning sun rather than afternoon sun.

You may also need to protect your plants from falling over in strong winds. If you have many pots they might provide some protection for each other. Place the tallest plants along walls or trellises.

And if you do have a trellis you can also try some climbing plants providing there is enough support. You might like to grow a passionfruit if you have a sunny wall. Or what about snow peas or sugar snap peas?

If space is really at a premium then you do really need to think about growing vertically. There are dwarf varieties of many fruit trees now that will happily grow in a good sized pot. You could espalier your fruit tree along a trellis if you have one.

Get creative. Hanging baskets could give you extra plant space for strawberries, cherry tomatoes or a basket brimming with herbs.

Many conventional gardeners find themselves with more than just a few plants growing in containers. I wouldn't think of any other way to grow mints as they are just impossible if they escape into the garden. And how many people have the space for a full grown bay tree, when they only use a few leaves each week?

Tips For Container Growing

- Use a premium potting mix
- Add a slow release organic fertilizer when you pot up your container
- Also add water crystals to help keep the soil moist
- Re-pot your plants each spring to encourage vigorous growth (add slow release fertilizer every spring when you re-pot)
- DO NOT OVERWATER – allow the soil surface to dry out between watering
- And DO NOT ALLOW TO DRY OUT

- Keep new growth trimmed to promote bushiness
- Choose a sunny position – at least 4-6 hours a day

Yes, container plants take a little extra care, but we are well rewarded with our bounties. Try growing a few pots together. They look great and they provide a suitable micro-climate for each other. Good luck with yours!

Organic Gardening Equipment & Supplies

"Conventional" garden supply centres now have many products that are suitable for organic gardeners, especially these days. However, I have found it more difficult to find organic seeds, less common varieties and heirloom varieties.

Your best option is to look online or in seed catalogues for seed suppliers that specialize in organic seeds – that way you'll know for sure that what you're buying has been grown, saved and stored organically as they will have organic certification.

Organic Food Profits

*A*s a beginner to organic gardening you probably won't have an excess of produce in your first growing season. If you have extra produce that you can't use fresh, you can try your hand at freezing, bottling, canning, dehydrating and storing.

If you still have an abundance of produce – well done. You are clearly an excellent gardener. Friends and neighbours will be delighted with any organic food you are willing to share with them.

If you decide you want to grow much more produce than your family can use, you'll be thinking about selling your excess. You need to research your country's laws for organic certification.

In most cases it takes three to four years of growing to strict organic regulations before you can be certified as organic. In the mean time you can still sell your produce, but you must not call it organic until you are legally certified, but you can say that it has been grown without chemicals.

Of course the main benefit in getting the rubber stamp for organic certification is that your customers have the security of knowing that you definitely grow organically and so you can ask a far greater price for your wonderful, healthy food.

There are many other ways to make money from your garden. Craft items are always a good seller at local markets. Be as creative as you can. You will be able to grow many of the things you might need to create gorgeous gifts.

You could create seasonal or holiday themes, such as gifts for valentine's day, mother's day, Halloween and Christmas. I'm sure you could come up with thousands of ideas.

More Organic Gardening Information

*A*dditional information about organic gardening may be found at my blog:

www.1stopOrganicGardening.com/blog

and

Join my <u>free</u> **Go Organic Club** and get weekly organic gardening articles, gifts, bonuses, reviews, and more at:

www.1stoporganicgardening.com/join.htm

Vegetable Sowing Chart for Southern Hemisphere

	Tropical / Sub-Tropical	Temperate	Cold
	J F M A M J J A S O N D	J F M A M J J A S O N D	J F M A M J J A S O N D
Artichoke, Globe	✓✓✓	✓✓✓✓✓	✓✓✓✓
Artichoke, Jerusalem	✓✓✓✓	✓✓✓	✓✓✓✓✓
Asparagus	✓✓✓	✓✓	✓✓
Bean (dwarf)	✓✓✓✓✓✓✓✓	✓✓ ✓✓✓✓	✓ ✓✓✓
Bean (climbing)	✓✓✓✓✓✓✓✓	✓ ✓✓✓✓	✓✓✓
Bean (broad)	✓✓✓	✓✓✓✓	✓✓ ✓✓
Beetroot	✓✓✓✓✓✓✓✓	✓✓✓ ✓✓✓✓✓	✓✓ ✓✓✓✓
Broccoli	✓✓✓✓✓	✓✓✓✓✓ ✓	✓✓ ✓✓
Brussels Sprouts		✓✓✓ ✓	✓✓ ✓✓✓
Cabbage	✓✓✓✓✓✓✓✓✓	✓✓✓✓ ✓✓✓✓✓✓	✓✓✓ ✓✓✓✓✓
Cabbage, Chinese	✓✓✓✓✓✓✓✓✓✓✓	✓✓✓✓ ✓✓✓✓✓✓	✓✓✓ ✓✓✓✓✓✓
Capsicum	✓✓✓ ✓✓✓✓✓✓	✓✓✓✓✓	✓✓✓
Carrots	✓✓✓✓✓✓✓✓✓✓	✓✓✓ ✓✓✓✓✓✓	✓✓ ✓✓✓✓
Cauliflower	✓✓✓✓	✓✓✓ ✓	✓ ✓✓
Celery	✓✓✓✓	✓✓ ✓✓✓✓✓	✓✓✓✓
Choko	✓✓✓✓	✓✓✓	
Corn	✓✓ ✓✓✓✓✓✓	✓ ✓✓✓✓	✓✓✓
Cucumber	✓✓✓ ✓✓✓✓✓✓	✓ ✓✓✓✓	✓✓✓
Eggplant	✓✓✓ ✓✓✓✓	✓✓✓✓	✓✓
Endive	✓✓✓✓✓✓	✓✓✓ ✓✓✓✓✓	✓✓ ✓✓✓✓
Kale		✓✓✓✓	✓✓✓✓✓ ✓✓
Kohlrabi	✓✓✓✓	✓✓✓ ✓✓✓	✓✓ ✓✓✓
Leek	✓✓✓	✓✓✓✓ ✓✓✓✓	✓✓✓ ✓✓✓
Lettuce	✓✓✓✓✓✓✓✓✓✓	✓✓✓✓✓✓✓✓✓✓✓	✓✓✓✓✓✓✓✓✓✓✓
Okra	✓✓ ✓✓✓✓✓	✓✓✓✓	✓✓✓
Onion	✓✓✓✓	✓✓✓✓✓	✓✓✓✓✓
Onion, spring	✓✓✓✓✓✓✓✓✓✓	✓✓✓✓✓ ✓✓✓✓✓	✓✓✓✓ ✓✓✓✓✓

Parsnip	✓✓✓✓✓	✓✓✓	✓✓✓✓✓	✓✓	✓✓✓✓✓
Pea (dwarf)	✓✓✓✓✓	✓✓✓✓✓✓			✓✓✓✓✓
Pea (climbing)	✓✓✓✓✓	✓✓✓✓✓✓✓			✓✓✓✓✓
Potato	✓✓✓✓✓✓✓	✓✓	✓✓✓		✓✓✓✓✓
Pumpkin	✓✓ ✓✓✓✓✓✓		✓✓✓✓		✓✓✓
Radish	✓✓✓✓✓✓✓✓✓✓	✓✓✓✓✓	✓✓✓✓✓	✓✓✓✓	✓✓✓✓
Rhubarb	✓✓✓✓		✓✓✓✓✓		✓✓✓✓
Shallot	✓✓✓✓✓✓	✓✓✓✓✓		✓✓✓✓✓	
Silverbeet	✓✓✓✓✓✓✓✓✓✓	✓✓✓	✓✓✓✓✓✓	✓✓	✓✓✓✓✓
Spinach	✓✓✓✓	✓✓✓✓✓		✓✓✓✓✓✓✓	
Squash	✓✓ ✓✓✓✓✓✓		✓✓✓✓		✓✓✓
Swede	✓✓✓	✓✓✓		✓✓	✓✓
Sweet Potato	✓✓ ✓✓✓✓✓✓		✓✓✓		
Tomato	✓✓✓✓✓✓✓✓✓✓		✓✓✓✓✓		✓✓✓
Turnip	✓✓✓✓	✓✓✓✓		✓✓✓	✓✓✓
Zucchini	✓✓✓ ✓✓✓✓✓✓	✓	✓✓✓✓		✓✓✓

Vegetable Sowing Chart for Northern Hemisphere

	Tropical / Sub-Tropical	Temperate	Cold
	J A S O N D J F M A M J	J A S O N D J F M A M J	J A S O N D J F M A M J
Artichoke, Globe	✓✓✓	✓✓✓✓✓	✓✓✓✓
Artichoke, Jerusalem	✓✓✓✓	✓✓✓	✓✓✓✓✓
Asparagus	✓✓✓	✓✓	✓✓
Bean (dwarf)	✓✓✓✓✓✓✓✓	✓✓ ✓✓✓✓	✓ ✓✓✓
Bean (climbing)	✓✓✓✓✓✓✓✓	✓ ✓✓✓✓	✓✓✓
Bean (broad)	✓✓✓	✓✓✓✓	✓✓ ✓✓
Beetroot	✓✓✓✓✓✓✓✓	✓✓✓ ✓✓✓✓✓	✓✓ ✓✓✓✓
Broccoli	✓✓✓✓✓✓	✓✓✓✓✓ ✓	✓✓ ✓✓
Brussels Sprouts		✓✓✓ ✓	✓✓ ✓✓
Cabbage	✓✓✓✓✓✓✓✓✓	✓✓✓✓ ✓✓✓✓✓✓	✓✓✓ ✓✓✓✓✓
Cabbage, Chinese	✓✓✓✓✓✓✓✓✓✓✓	✓✓✓✓ ✓✓✓✓✓✓	✓✓✓ ✓✓✓✓✓
Capsicum	✓✓✓ ✓✓✓✓✓	✓✓✓✓✓	✓✓✓
Carrots	✓✓✓✓✓✓✓✓✓✓✓	✓✓✓ ✓✓✓✓✓✓	✓✓ ✓✓✓✓
Cauliflower	✓✓✓✓	✓✓✓ ✓	✓ ✓✓
Celery	✓✓✓	✓✓ ✓✓✓✓✓	✓✓✓✓
Choko	✓✓✓✓	✓✓✓	
Corn	✓✓ ✓✓✓✓✓✓	✓ ✓✓✓✓	✓✓✓
Cucumber	✓✓✓ ✓✓✓✓✓✓	✓ ✓✓✓✓	✓✓✓
Eggplant	✓✓✓ ✓✓✓✓	✓✓✓✓	✓✓
Endive	✓✓✓✓✓✓	✓✓✓ ✓✓✓✓✓	✓✓ ✓✓✓✓
Kale		✓✓✓✓	✓✓✓✓✓ ✓✓
Kohlrabi	✓✓✓✓	✓✓✓ ✓✓✓	✓✓ ✓✓✓
Leek	✓✓✓	✓✓✓✓ ✓✓✓✓	✓✓✓ ✓✓✓
Lettuce	✓✓✓✓✓✓✓✓✓✓✓	✓✓✓✓✓✓✓✓✓✓✓	✓✓✓✓✓✓✓✓✓✓✓
Okra	✓✓ ✓✓✓✓✓	✓✓✓	✓✓✓
Onion	✓✓✓✓	✓✓✓✓✓	✓✓✓✓
Onion, spring	✓✓✓✓✓✓✓✓✓✓	✓✓✓✓✓ ✓✓✓✓✓	✓✓✓✓ ✓✓✓✓✓

Parsnip	✓✓✓✓✓	✓✓✓ ✓✓✓✓✓✓	✓✓ ✓✓✓✓✓
Pea (dwarf)	✓✓✓✓✓	✓✓✓✓✓✓✓	✓✓✓✓✓
Pea (climbing)	✓✓✓✓✓	✓✓✓✓✓✓✓	✓✓✓✓✓
Potato	✓✓✓✓✓✓✓	✓✓ ✓✓✓	✓✓✓✓✓
Pumpkin	✓✓ ✓✓✓✓✓	✓✓✓✓	✓✓✓
Radish	✓✓✓✓✓✓✓✓✓✓✓	✓✓✓✓ ✓✓✓✓	✓✓✓✓ ✓✓✓✓
Rhubarb	✓✓✓✓	✓✓✓✓✓	✓✓✓✓
Shallot	✓✓✓✓✓✓	✓✓✓✓✓	✓✓✓✓✓
Silverbeet	✓✓✓✓✓✓✓✓✓✓✓	✓✓✓ ✓✓✓✓✓✓	✓✓ ✓✓✓✓✓
Spinach	✓✓✓✓	✓✓✓✓✓	✓✓✓✓✓✓✓✓
Squash	✓✓ ✓✓✓✓✓✓	✓✓✓✓	✓✓✓
Swede	✓✓✓	✓✓✓	✓✓ ✓✓
Sweet Potato	✓✓ ✓✓✓✓✓✓	✓✓✓	
Tomato	✓✓✓✓✓✓✓✓✓✓✓	✓✓✓✓✓	✓✓✓
Turnip	✓✓✓✓	✓✓✓✓	✓✓ ✓✓✓
Zucchini	✓✓✓ ✓✓✓✓✓✓	✓ ✓✓✓✓	✓✓✓

*T*his final section is compiled from some questions that have been emailed to me from people who had bought this book and wanted a little more specific information to help them out. Their questions may help you too.

Question from Taryn Perna

Q: Is compost tea better than compost, is it used together or instead of regular compost and how do I make it?

A: OK, compost verses compost tea. Compost tea is mostly used as a foliar spray to give plants a bit of a pep-me-up. Any plants that are not looking all that happy might benefit from a spray of compost tea. You don't want to overdo foliar spraying though. Every two to four weeks should be plenty. See what you are essentially doing is forcing the plant to eat, but now and then can be beneficial.

To make a compost tea you take some compost that you've made (or bought), place a shovel full or so in a permeable bag (or old pillowcase) and sit it in a tub full of water to seep for a few weeks. Collect some of the tea water in a jug. If it's really dark you need to dilute it with water til it looks like tea - that's why it's called compost tea. Then just spray onto the leaves of your plants.

Mostly I just add mature compost to the top of my soil and let the worms do their work, rather than turn it into tea. Give it a go though.

I hope this answers your question.

Kind regards,
Julie

Note: read the chapter on making your own liquid fertilizers on page 50

Question from Luke Scobie

Q: When I buy organic vegetables they tend to last 3-5 days, yet when I take vegetables out of my garden they only last a few hours before they wilt and go all soft if I don't refrigerate them immediately.

So am I doing something wrong or is that just the way it is or do I need to pick them at certain times or store them a certain way? – I know it's a pretty generic question but I am struggling with it, as I would rather go pick for a few days at a time.

Cheers.

A: Hi Luke, thanks for your question.

Yes, your organic veggies picked from the garden will wilt if you don't treat them well.

My first tip is to pick them either first thing in the morning, or late in the evening as the sun's going down. It will help even more if you have watered your garden an hour or two before you start picking.

Secondly, you really should refrigerate your produce. Some things do better in plastic bags or containers, such as most greens and root vegetables.

These two tips will make a big difference in how long your vegetables will stay fresh, but I think you can't beat picking your meal just before you prepare it to eat. The "life energy" if you like, is still in the plant. I believe when you ingest your food still alive you are adding greatly to your general well being (but maybe that's just me!).

I hope this helps - give it a try and see how you go.

Kind regards,
Julie

Question from Shanda Ayala

Q: I've already read the beginners manual its wonderful. I've always wanted to garden but never knew where to even start thank you for the knowledge.

I have a question about the compost, because things I have on hand now are not organic, will that contaminate my compost? There thing for the grocery store I don't know what might be on them.

Thank You
Shanda Ayala

A: Hi Shanda, glad you love the manual and that it will help you get started. Sometimes getting started is the hardest part, but I think if you can do even just 1 little thing in your garden each day it really adds up over a year. You might surprise yourself!

I would add anything that once came to the earth into my compost. I even throw in mice that I catch in traps and animals that die. They all add to the mineral content of the compost. Don›t worry too much that you don›t know the life of veggies and other things from the supermarket. One of the real beauties of a compost heap is that almost every toxic nasty is broken down in the composting process. I wouldn›t add shiny print advertising, but anything that comes off your dinner plate is fine. After all, you›ve already eaten the bulk of it before you throw out your scraps.

I hope this helps put your mind at ease. Create yourself a wonderful veggie garden so that you need to buy from elsewhere less and less. That way you can be sure you›re eating organic.

Kind regards,
Julie

Question from Wendy Hollender

Q: I have a cold house for winter harvesting. It is doing great. I live in Ulster County. Only problem is the field mouse are having a field day inside, eating everything. Any ideas on how to keep them out?

Thanks for your help!

Regards,
Wendy

A: Hi Wendy, thanks for your question. I'm not sure that this will be much help, but I personally use traps when mice appear. I prefer to use the plastic type that you can't catch your own fingers in when setting them. You use peanut butter to attract them.

I know in Australia you can get an electrical device that emits a high pitch frequency (above human range) that repels mice and rats. Dick Smith Electronics in Australia stocks them. Don't know if they retail in the US, but you should be able to get them in a major electrical retail store or electrical hobbyist type store.

These are the only options that I can think of that don't resort to chemicals. Of course you could also try getting a really hungry cat. ☺

Kind regards,
Julie

Question from Lauretha Whaley

Q: Very interested in planning and creating organic garden – what is best time (season) to start to prepare soil for garden? I live in Columbia South Carolina and I anticipate starting with a summer garden and eventually move on to an all season or at least three season garden.

A: Hi Lauretha, thanks for your question. Preparing the soil is an ongoing process, so don't get too caught up in getting it perfect straight away. I like to prepare the most each spring by adding organic compost to the soil surface (no digging). If you don't have your own compost most garden landscaping supply centres have it. Even if you can't get compost at all, you can just start out with using organic fertilizer pellets around your plants and add an organic mulch to the surface (like pea straw or similar). As it breaks down over the summer it will add food and structure to the soil.

It takes time to create really good, rich, humus-filled soil – lots of years, but if you keep adding organic matter it happens. That's why having your own compost heap is such a beneficial part of organic gardening and your keeping your waste out of the system... an added bonus.

If you haven't grown a veggie garden before, I'd also suggest starting out with a small plot first, maybe 3 or 4 yards by 1 yard and manage that for a while. Or you could do two that size along side each other. Making the plots narrow means you don't need to step in your plot to reach things and that way you're not compacting the soil.

I hope this helps.

Kind regards,
Julie

Question from Jean Newbold

Q: Hi Julie, I'm going for my lifelong dream - a small homestead in south central Pennsylvania, USA. I want to go organic but this place has been farmed with chemicals for four generations.

My garden will be on a conventionally farmed piece of land. I propose to plant cover crops and sheet compost the garden to build fertility. How can I get rid of the chemical fertilizers and pesticides, etc., in the ground and approximately how long will it take?

A: Hmmm.... that's a bit of a tricky question. It depends on how big an area you're considering growing organically on. Unless you get the soil analysed you won't know what chemicals have been applied and whether they have a residual effect or not.

Most fertilizers are leeched through the soil til there's virtually nothing left - that's why they have to re-apply them every season. So if you live in an area with lots of rain fall it probably isn't a huge issue as the rain creates the leeching effect.

Things you can do to turn the soil into a whole, living organism again include growing cover crops like you've suggested. Adding large amounts of organic matter will create better and better soil. With better soil you'll be creating an environment which will attract worms and micro-organisms back into the soil.

I don't think there is a quick and easy solution - but if you continue to add compost and organic matter to the soil, it will continue to improve.

Just to let you know... most of us start out with soil that has probably had chemicals on it at some stage. The best we can do is keep improving it over time. My big tip would be to start out working on a manageable size plot first and then work your way up to bigger and bigger areas.

I hope this helps you a little. Good luck with your garden.

Kind regards,
Julie

Question from Deanna Osborne

Q: Julie, I would like to know where on the beet plant are the seeds to grow more beets found? I hope you have the answer. Thank you. I am trying to save my own seeds for next year.

A: Hi Deanna, when your beetroot flowers (late summer) it will produce seed (where the flowers fall off). They are sort of corky, like spinach or silverbeet if you know what they look like. There are usually 4 seeds or so in a cluster. The cluster just looks like a single seed. Let your seeds dry on the flower stalk or they may not mature.

Next spring when you want to plant them, just soak the clusters overnight – it helps them germinate as the water soaks right in before you get them in the soil.

I hope this helps,

Kind regards,
Julie

Question from Tina Clark

Q: Hi Julie, I am having a lot of trouble with my cauliflower and broccoli - there are aphids and then some green caterpillar looking things eating the leaves. What would you suggest?
I live in Sydney.

Thanks so much.
Tina

A: Hi Tina, Brassicas can be really tricky to grow pest free (organically). I've seen people grow them with closely woven netting, so that sunshine and water still get to the plants, but the insects can't. I'm not sure if this would work for aphids, but it does prevent the cabbage moth from laying its eggs on your brassicas and then having the caterpillars devouring them.

You could pick the caterpillars off by hand, but this is quite time consuming and you're bound to miss a few.

Hope this helps,

Kind regards,
Julie

Question from Jon Meier

Q: Hi Julie, I am going to try a no-dig extension to my current garden for next year. I am already using the spot for placing my experimental jug plants. The layer is just grass. Next Spring I will enhance the spot with a layer of compost.

I will probably plant small/short plants as I depend entirely on the southern sun and grow the tallest plants (ie. sunflowers) in the back followed by tomatoes, then peppers and eggplant. Do you have any additional comments or suggestions?

On a different topic, I don›t have as much room as I would like in my garden so I am always trying to make use of my space.

Next year I wanted to try an alternate version of the Three Sisters Method except instead of corn I would grow sunflowers to attract pollinators and provide a climb for small cucumbers (in lieu of beans).

I found that cukes have no problems hanging as I never had one fall of the vine this year. For the ground cover I will have melons.

Again, Do you have any additional comments or suggestions?

I plan on sowing legumes over my whole garden in the fall for nitrogen. I found that any dried bean from the market will grow so I would like to know which of the popular store beans are best. I have red, white, black, pinto.....

FYI, Pepper plants do well in a gallon jug (see pic below).

Jon

A: Hi Jon, thanks for your email & photos. Suggestions? Anywhere you're creating a no-dig garden over grass (depending on what kind of grass really) you need to use quite a few layers to be sure that your grass doesn't end up coming up through all your vegetables, creating a big weeding problem.

The only problem I can see with growing members of the cucurbit family close together is if you want to save seed. There's a fair chance that your flowers will cross pollinate, so your seed will be hybrids of the two plants. Probably not in a good way. ☺

As for the beans for nitrogen – it doesn't really matter what kind you use. If you know other gardeners in the area you could ask them which ones grow best in your area. Other than that I'd just buy the cheapest as your going to cut them down as soon as they start to flower anyway. You might want to add some organic fertilizer pellets to the cut beans if your going to just let them lie on the ground (no-dig) and cover it all with some mulch as the warmer weather arrives. Hope this helps…

Kind regards,
Julie

Question from Stuart C

Q: Hi Julie, I have been receiving your newsletter for several months now and I enjoy them very much. But in your latest newsletter you talk of pest control and how to avoid them.

One of the suggestions you give is to «grow disease resistant varieties

Now I can only interpret this as genetically modified plants.

Are you promoting the idea that we begin to plant genetically modified crops? I could give you endless days of proof of the horrors of these, so I will allow you to answer and hope that this is a misunderstanding.

Stuart.

A: Hi Stuart, thanks for writing with your concern. No, I'm not talking about genetically modified plants – the idea is abhorrent to me too. Let me clarify. I'm talking about plant selection. Choosing the strongest, healthiest, highest yielding plants to save seeds from.

Just like in the rest of nature – survival of the fittest if you will, but with a little thought thrown in for good measure. So please be rest assured that I'm not talking about gene splicing or anything remotely like it – just natural selection.

I hope this puts your mind at ease.

Kind regards,
Julie

Question from Bethany Farah

Q: I've really been wanting to grow some scarlet runner beans for such a long time. But then I learned that squirrels love to eat bean pole seedlings and we had one move into the neighborhood recently (he's made a snack of my cucumber leaves) and I'm worried about him eating my poor seedlings.

I also noticed that you mentioned in a blog that scarlet runner beans are perennial. Is that really true? How can i be sure mine come back year after year? (I live in usda zone 9) And exactly how big do they get because I'm worried about not having a big enough trellis.

Speaking of trellises, do you have any suggestions on where to get/ make one for dirt cheap; almost free dirt cheap? Any other tips will be greatly appreciated.

Novice gardener,
Bethany Farah

A: Hi Bethany, we don't have squirrels in Australia – just possums... They love to eat new growth on many food plants and roses too.

Scarlet runner beans are perennial. They grow in spring, flower and produce pods through summer, then die off. In the next spring they should burst through the soil again and repeat the process over. You have to make sure you get scarlet runner bean seeds to plant out.

My trellis is about 6 foot tall and it really could have been taller. They grew about 2 or 3 feet taller than the trellis and sort of just hang about.

As for a cheap trellis… I just used 2 x 9' tall star droppers (steel posts) and tied trellis wire to them. It works well and is easy to do and quite cheap, especially if you have the droppers already. Hope this helps,

Kind regards,
Julie

Question from Jasbir Jandaur

Q: Hi Julie , thanks for helping me by sending me tips for for gardening, as I am just new in this field. This year I'm just learning how to grow. I'm learning from reading on internet on different websites.

I used horse manure compost, and noticed that plants not growing much in size and volume, and looks like it has got some burning effect as well. In my indoor veg plants like pepper and chilly are very small in size and no fruit at all. Could you please guide me how to use compost. Thankyou!

Many Regards
Jasbir

A: If I understand what you've said, you used horse manure compost to grow your veggies in. Usually you would use a good potting mix and just add compost (of any kind) as a mulch or top-dressing.

If the manure was not composted completely it will most likely burn your plants. It must be completely composted to use on any plants. The other thing is that it sounds like you've not created a well balanced compost.

You need to incorporate many different ingredients in your compost to supply a good mix of nutrients to your plants. I hope this helps a little.

Kind regards,
Julie

Question from Janemarie Smith

Q: I have planted peas a month ago. The plants are about 5" in height and quite hearty looking. However, I see no signs of pods.

Can you please shed some light on when these plants show signs of the pea pods?

A: You haven't said what your location / season is, but peas will take a little longer than a month to start growing pods.

They are usually at least 4 or 5 foot tall before flowering (pretty white flowers). The pea pods form from where the flower grew, so don't pick the flowers. You probably won't be eating peas for at least 8 to 10 weeks after you planted them.

Hope this helps,

Kind regards,
Julie

Question from Liam Lawless

Q: Hi Julie, if I am out of order by asking questions, I apologise so please tell me so.

Tip 1. When growing carrots sprinkle coffee grounds around them to deter the carrot fly.

Tip 2. To prevent slugs from devouring your produce push small containers into the soil to ground level with beer in them. Slugs prefer the beer and will pass by your produce to get to the beer. (I use Guinness that I get from our local pub for free. It is the slops and spillage that would otherwise be thrown out) What a good way to recycle. By the way the slugs are so greedy for the beer they get drunk and drown. They do however, have a smile on their faces when they die.

Question 1. I have access to lots of seaweed that is washed up on the beach. I am thinking of collecting it and shredding into pellets. Would you think this would be good for my soil?

Question 2. I have access to horse and cow manure, is one better than the other for growing vegetables?

Julie, just delete the tips if you already know of them.

Best wishes,
Liam

A: Hi Liam, thanks for your tips - it's always good to hear tips from other gardeners.

Seaweed is an excellent organic additive to your garden. Trouble is I believe it›s illegal to collect it (at least it is in Australia), so don›t get caught. The other thing to consider is that it is covered in salt. You don›t want to have this go on your garden, so you›ll need to wash the salt off before using it.

And the cow or horse manure: I think they are both good for your veggies, once composted (or matured). Something to consider (again) is how the animals have been fed and if they›ve been given antibiotics and/or hormones. But if you compost it before use on your garden, the composting process will break it down to it›s most natural composition.

I hope this helps...

Kind regards,
Julie

Thank you for purchasing my book. I hope it has inspired you to create your own productive organic food garden.

Join my <u>free</u> Go Organic Club and get weekly organic gardening articles, gifts, bonuses, reviews, and more at:

www.1stoporganicgardening.com/join.htm

and
You will find more tips and ongoing posts on my blog:
www.1stoporganicgardening.com/blog

Love and Blessings to you,
Julie

24880296R00068

Made in the USA
Lexington, KY
04 August 2013